Muddy Boots and Ragged Aprons

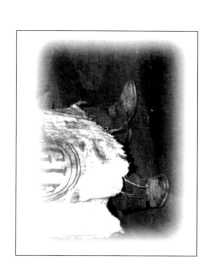

# MUDDY BOOTS AND RAGGED APRONS

Images of Working-Class Detroit, 1900-1930

KEVIN BOYLE & VICTORIA GETIS

Wayne State University Press  Detroit

00 99 98 97                                                        5 4 3 2 1

**Library of Congress Cataloging-in-Publication Data**

Boyle, Kevin, 1960-
   Muddy boots and ragged aprons : Images of working-class Detroit,
1900-1930 / Kevin Boyle and Victoria Getis.
       p.      cm.
   Includes bibliographical references (p.      ).
   ISBN 0-8143-2482-7 (pbk. : alk. paper)
   1. Working class—Michigan—Detroit—History. 2. Detroit (Mich.)—
Social conditions.   I. Getis, Victoria, 1966-    . II. Title.
HD8085.D6B69   1997
305.5'62'0977434—dc20
                                                              96-28256

Note: Under an agreement with the Ford Motor Company, names obtained from
the company have been changed to protect the privacy of the individuals. Names
that have been changed are marked with an asterisk the first time they appear. In
changing names, we have attempted to make the altered name conform to the
original in terms of ethnicity. Names obtained from other sources have not been
changed.

*Front cover photo credits:* (left) Ford Motor Company Industrial Archives, acc. AR-
84-57033, photo 308; (center) Ford Motor Company Industrial Archives, acc. AR-
57033, photo 416; (right) Burton Historical Collection of the Detroit Public Library,
Harvey C. Jackson Collection. *Back cover photo credits:* (left) Archdiocese of
Detroit Archives, League of Catholic Women Collection, Box 51; (top right) Henry
Ford Museum and Greenfield Village; (bottom right) Archdiocese of Detroit
Archives, St.Rose of Lima Collection, Box 11. For additional photo credits, see
p. 207.

# Contents

# Acknowledgments

We would like to extend our deepest thanks to the Tolkacz family, whose story opens *Muddy Boots and Ragged Aprons*. The Tolkacz family—the late Joseph; his wife, Betty; their son, Joe; and Joe's wife, Nancy—enriched this book immeasurably, as they have enriched our lives for the last twenty years. We are also grateful to Charles Trierweiler, who repeatedly pushed us to put this book together. Without his encouragement, we might never have started or completed the project.

The book has its origins in research work undertaken for David L. Lewis at the University of Michigan. One of the first steps we took to make this book a reality was to contact Philip Mason, then the director of the Archives of Labor and Urban Affairs at Wayne State University. He endorsed our idea and put us in touch with Arthur Evans of Wayne State University Press. The Press sought a review of the book proposal from John Barnard, who wrote an enthusiastic assessment. We would also like to thank an anonymous reviewer for the Press. We have also like to thank for fostering *Muddy Boots and Ragged Aprons*.

Thanks are due as well to the many archivists and librarians who assisted us. Darleen Flaherty of the Ford Industrial Archives provided critical support in our securing permission to use the Ford Motor Company photos. She also provided background material on the photos themselves. William Buffa of Ford granted permission to use the Ford photos. Roman Godzak of the Roman Catholic Archdiocese of Detroit was a helpful guide to the archdiocese's holdings and was full of information about the history of Detroit churches. Pamela VanOverbeke showed us the ropes at the Manning Brothers Commercial Photography archives. David Perimba made the Burton Library manageable; he was also a font of information about the Detroit Tigers and the Ernie Harwell collection. It was a pleasure to work with Luke J. Gilliland-Swetland at the Ford Historical Museum at Greenfield Village; Terry Hoover also aided our search there. The staff of the *Detroit News* library were knowledgeable and friendly guides to the newspaper's holdings, and Jeanette Bartz helped us secure the

# Acknowledgments

photos we needed. Nancy Bartlett of the Michigan Historical Collections at the Bentley Library helped scour the archives for appropriate photos. Finally, Thomas Featherstone, of the Archives for Labor and Urban Affairs, Wayne State University, provided photos from his own collection, showed us little-known photos in the library collection, and lent us photography equipment. Many thanks to all of these archivists and the institutions they represent.

Some of the photos were acquired with funds provided by a summer faculty fellowship from the University of Toledo. Our thanks to the Department of History and the College of Arts and Sciences at the University of Toledo for their support.

*Muddy Boots and Ragged Aprons* is in large part a book about families. It is also a product of families, the families that made us into the people we are today and the family we are now building. This book is dedicated to them all: Our parents, Arthur and Judith Getis and Kevin and Anne Boyle; our siblings and in-laws, Hilary and Jamal Tarazi, Anne and Anthony Tibbetts, and Brian and Kathy Boyle; our nieces and nephews, Sophie and Christina Tarazi and Brian, Elizabeth, Evan, and Sarah Boyle; and our other joint projects, Abigail and Hannah Boyle.

*The wedding portrait of Anthonina Sergej and Simon Tolkacz, July 1911.*

# Introduction

On July 25, 1911, Simon Tolkacz and Anthonina Sergej, kneeling in the great sanctuary of Detroit's Immaculate Conception Church, publicly professed their love and commitment. At 27, Simon had already experienced a lifetime of change. Born to a farming family in eastern Poland, he had escaped being drafted into the Russian army by slipping across the border into Germany. He then joined the thousands of Poles who, each week, left Central Europe for Ellis Island. The year was 1903; Simon was 19.[1]

Over the next four years, he worked his way westward from New York, first as a farm laborer, then as a miner in Pennsylvania. In 1907, he made his final move—to Detroit, where the burgeoning auto industry offered steady work at reasonable wages. There he found a job as a laborer in the foundry of the Ford auto production plant. It was brutally hard work. "The air [in the foundry] during working hours," according to one observer, "cannot be endured by any work-

man save those possessing respiratory organs of the most robust description." Outside the plant, though, Simon found his solace; he found Anthonina. Seven years his junior, she too had grown up in eastern Poland. Unlike Simon, she had left her homeland for romantic reasons: all of Poland's most eligible bachelors, she told her family, were now in America.[2]

Anthonina was a strong-willed woman, and she soon began to shape the couple's life together. She hated seeing her husband return from the foundry drenched in sweat and covered in coal dust, and she urged him to find other work. When she became pregnant in 1912, she also insisted that they move from the rooms they had rented above Stanley Sudol's Saloon in the city's Polish section, on the lower east side. Spurred by his wife, Simon built a four-room house on Sargent Street, a few blocks away. And he found a new and more pleasant job, on the loading dock of the nearby Dodge Main plant.[3]

The Tolkaczs had five children—two sons and three

daughters—in seven years, and Simon simply could not earn enough to keep his children fed, clothed, and in school. Anthonina supplemented his income by taking in boarders; for years, the Tolkacz family shared its four rooms with six single, Polish-born autoworkers. In the end, the couple's struggles paid off: all five children finished high school; their sons became skilled workers, and their daughters married well.[4]

*Muddy Boots and Ragged Aprons* is about Simon and Anthonina and a million people like them—working people who in the first three decades of the twentieth century made Detroit into one of the world's greatest industrial cities. It traces the fabric of their lives: at home and at work, in school and in neighborhood stores, at play and at prayer. Unlike many historical studies, however, the book tells its story through photographs, drawn from a range of public and private sources. It invites readers to enter the lives of Detroit's workers, to see the world as they lived it, and as they changed it.

In the second half of the nineteenth century, the American economy underwent a dramatic transformation. At the beginning of the Civil War, the United States was still an overwhelmingly agricultural country: four of five Americans made their living off the land. By 1900, the United States had become the world's foremost industrial power, easily outstripping Great Britain, its nearest rival. No part of the nation remained unaffected; as the twentieth century began, Americans labored in the steel mills of Alabama, the oil fields of Texas, and the sweatshops of San Francisco. The heart of industrial America, though, lay in a corridor of northeastern and midwestern cities, extending from New York, Philadelphia, and Boston, through Buffalo, Pittsburgh, and Cleveland, to Chicago and St. Louis.[5]

To maintain this vast complex of factories, mills, and shops, industrialists required millions of workers, many skilled in particular trades such as carpentry and iron molding, many more with no skills save the stamina to endure long hours and brutal working conditions. Industry's demand for labor, in turn, triggered massive shifts in population. In part, the movement was internal. Between 1865 and 1900, millions of Americans, black and white, left their farms for the factories. It was more common for American industry to draw its workers from beyond the United States, however. In the latter half of the nineteenth century, fourteen million immigrants poured into the country in search of work, and in the process they fundamentally altered the face of urban America.[6]

Prior to industrialization, the United States had been populated largely by white Anglo-Saxon Protestants, African Americans, and Native Americans. The immigrants of the late nineteenth century, in contrast, came primarily from Poland, Russia, the Austro-Hungarian Empire, Greece, Italy, and the other nations of southern and eastern Europe. Speaking no English, dressed in traditional clothes, carrying all their possessions in a few suitcases, immigrants often struck native-born Americans as little more than the Old World's "wretched refuse." Employers, however, welcomed the newcomers as a seemingly endless source of unskilled laborers. Immigrants thus crowded into the cities of the industrial belt; in 1900, 35 percent of Chicago's citizens and 37 percent of New York's citizens were foreign-born. In these cities, immigrants did their best to recreate the world they had left behind, building Catholic churches and Jewish synagogues, opening ethnic stores and social clubs, publishing foreign-language newspapers. Writing in 1876, the Polish author Henryk Sienkiewicz captured the texture of life in the Polish neighborhoods of Chicago. "The morning sun rising from the waters of Lake Michigan," he wrote, "illuminated Polish inscriptions and names on the buildings. . . . Doors and windows began to open . . . and the first words I heard were uttered in Polish. A few minutes later I caught sight of the Church of St. Stanislaus Kostka. . . . About eight o'clock in the morning flocks of children began to swarm here on the way to the school maintained by the priests and situated beside the church."[7]

The industrialization process had already swept through Detroit by 1900. In 1865, Detroit had been a frontier town with a population of 45,000. Forty years later, it was a major manufacturing center of 285,000, the nation's thirteenth largest city. As in other northeastern cities, immigrants accounted for most of the population growth; according to the best available study, 77 percent of all Detroiters were either foreign-born or the children of foreign-born parents in 1900. Together, industrialists and the workers they attracted made the city into a patchwork of factories and ethnic neighborhoods. Employers built their shops either along the riverfront or, increasingly, in the northern end of town, near the intersection of Woodward Avenue, the major north-south artery, and East Grand Boulevard. Workers filled in the remainder of the city, carving it into a series of tight-knit ethnic enclaves. Detroit's large

German population dominated the city's east side, particularly along Gratiot Avenue; the growing Polish population settled in the northeast, north of the German neighborhood; and the Russian-Jewish population settled to their west, along Hastings Street; African Americans—a minuscule 1.5 percent of the population—were increasingly segregated into a narrow band of streets on the eastern edge of downtown; and the Irish controlled the lower west side, along Michigan Avenue, though their hold on the area was already slipping. Few of these areas fit the stereotype of an ethnic ghetto. They were not crowded with multistory tenements, nor were their streets crammed with pushcarts. Most of Detroit's ethnic neighborhoods, rather, were lined with small, single-family homes. Detroit's immigrant workers, in fact, were more likely to own their own homes than were the city's native-born whites.[8]

As they were wont to do, civic boosters continually pointed to Detroit's expansion as proof of the city's economic vitality. "Talk of business depression passes over Detroit as lightly as water from a duck," a typical promoter proclaimed. "The goods [Detroit's businesses] produce are better constructed and better finished than those of almost any other city that might be mentioned." There was something to those claims, of course; Detroit's manufacturers and workers did produce an unusually large number of goods requiring skilled labor. In 1900, though, Detroit's economy was largely driven by the demand of its larger neighbors, such as Cleveland, Buffalo, and Chicago. For the most part, Detroit's plants supplied those cities with the hardware or machinery that their much larger factories needed to produce or distribute finished products. At the turn of the century, more than a quarter of Detroit's workers labored in the metal trade, producing castings, sheet metal, valves, and pipes, and the city's largest employer, American Car and Foundry built railroad cars for the Chicago market. For all its rapid growth, then, until 1900 Detroit remained in the second tier of industrial cities, an adjunct to, rather than a driving force of, the nation's economy.[9]

Then the automobile came to Detroit.

It is impossible to overestimate the impact the auto industry had on the American economy. When Ransom Olds opened Detroit's first auto factory in 1899, automobiles were still largely a novelty; in that year, automakers produced four thousand cars, virtually all of which were sold to the wealthy. Thirty years later, auto manufacturing had become the nation's dominant industry, mass producing five million cars and trucks for sale to rich and poor alike. In the process, the industry consumed a staggering amount of raw material—it was the nation's largest consumer of steel, rubber, and glass—and created a massive number of new jobs. Almost half a million men and women worked for auto manufacturers in 1929, and countless others, perhaps one in every six Americans, worked for firms dependent on auto manufacturing. The auto industry, in other words, had the power to make or break the American economy. All that power centered in Detroit.[10]

Historians offer a number of reasons why the auto industry developed in Detroit, such as the city's concentration of metalworkers and its access to the Great Lakes. In this case, however, causes are much less important than results. In a

very short time, the auto industry's extraordinary success transformed Detroit into one of the world's greatest industrial cities. By 1930, Detroit had 1.5 million inhabitants, five times its population in 1900. The city covered 139 square miles, more than three times its area in 1900. And its factories produced two billion dollars' worth of goods, more than any other American city except New York and Chicago.[11]

The new auto plants spread throughout Detroit, invading residential neighborhoods, filling vacant lots, choking the city with smoke and dirt. Studebaker and Timken Axle built their factories on the riverfront; Packard located on East Grand Boulevard; and Dodge and Briggs chose the city of Hamtramck, on the near east side. Continental, Hudson, and Chalmers staked out the far east side. Paige, Lincoln, and Kelsey Wheel the far west side. More than any other producer, however, the Ford Motor Company dominated the Detroit landscape. In 1904–5, Ford established its first large plant just south of Grand Boulevard, traditionally an industrial center. Four years later, the company moved production north, to Highland Park, where the automaker built what was then the world's largest industrial plant, the mammoth "Crystal Palace." Even that quickly proved insufficient, so in the late 1910s Ford began expanding the company's River Rouge complex, making the site, on the western edge of Detroit, into an industrial city of unparalleled size. By 1926, the Rouge covered 1,115 acres, maintained ninety-three miles of railroad track and twenty-seven miles of conveyors, and employed seventy-five thousand men and women.[12]

Detroit's auto factories were not simply the nation's largest and most important production plants; they were also the most innovative. At the turn of the century, auto work was skilled work: a group of tradesmen built each car from the ground up. It was an expensive and inefficient system; in 1910 it took more than twelve man-hours to assemble a single chassis. In the early 1900s, automakers, led by machinist Henry Ford, began trying to streamline the production process. By 1914, the Ford Motor Company had perfected its system. The company broke the process into a series of small tasks, mechanized those tasks as thoroughly as possible, then placed them side by side along an automated line. It was a brilliant innovation. Because the system was mechanized, Ford could turn most of its production work over to unskilled laborers, rather than relying on tradesmen. Ford workers therefore required virtually no training; company spokesmen bragged that they could turn an unskilled worker into a "first-class" factory hand in three days. Once on the job, workers exerted virtually no control over the system. Company officials determined precisely how fast they worked simply by setting the speed of the assembly line. Productivity—and profits—skyrocketed.[13]

In fact, Ford's system had only one major flaw. Workers found life on the assembly line terribly difficult. "[W]orkers cease to be human beings as soon as they enter the gates of the shop," one Ford worker explained. "They become automatons and cease to think. They move their arms spontaneously to and fro. . . . Many healthy workers have gone to work for Ford and have come home human wrecks." Factory hands responded to the pressure by quitting; the year after Ford installed its assembly line, the company had a turnover rate of 370 percent.[14]

In January 1914 Ford countered the labor turnover problem by doubling the workers' pay, from $2.50 to $5.00 a day. The company did so in a peculiar way, however, marrying industrial efficiency with paternalism. Workers applied for the pay raise; to certify them, the Ford Motor Company subjected each man to an investigation. Women were not eligible for the new wage, as the company intended the five dollar day for the breadwinners in a family; it considered women's work merely supplementary to the family economy. As part of the investigation, employees filled out forms answering questions about their habits, families, and financial situations. Ford investigators questioned family members, neighbors, and landlords, they examined bank books and living conditions. The company rewarded employees exhibiting sobriety, thriftiness, and the work ethic.[15] Investigators took photos of the homes of the workers, some of which are displayed in this book.

The maneuver worked. Ford's turnover rate plummeted, and its profits continued to rise. Other automakers soon followed his example, automating their plants and boosting their wages. And that, in turn, made Detroit a magnet for unskilled workers, who now saw in the auto industry an escape from grinding poverty, if not from the incessant demands of factory life. For many laborers, an observer declared, Detroit had become "an earthly Paradise, the color of smokey grey."[16]

The workers who poured into Detroit in the 1910s and 1920s did not fit any single mold. As in the late nineteenth century, the majority of newcomers came from eastern and southern

Europe. Most of these immigrants were Poles, who by 1920 had become the second largest group of European immigrants, followed by Italians, Hungarians, Slavs, and Greeks. When World War I blocked European immigration, white and black southerners streamed into Detroit to fill the void; according to Detroit Urban League records, more than a thousand African Americans arrived in Detroit each week in 1920. Throughout the 1910s and 1920s, workers from poorer-paying northern industries, and even from the factories of Britain and Germany, made their way to Detroit.[17]

Once in the city, workers immediately began looking for work, not an easy task even in the best of times. Frank Marquardt's first experience at a factory gate is fairly typical. The American-born son of a German steelworker and his wife, Marquardt was fifteen years old in January 1914 when he arrived in Detroit from Braddock, Pennsylvania, hoping to land one of the precious jobs at Ford. "I will [n]ever forget the sight that greeted us when we walked toward the Ford employment office," he recalled years later. "There were thousands of job seekers jam-packed in front of the gates. It was a bitterly cold morning and I had no overcoat, only a red sweater under a thin jacket. I don't know how long we stood in that crowd, but I became numb from the cold." Despite his difficult first encounter, Marquardt was lucky. Although he was not hired at Ford, he did secure a job in the auto industry, filing castings at the Metal Products Company, a parts supplier. That is not particularly surprising. Marquardt was young, white, and male; he spoke English, and he was familiar with factory life—precisely the attributes the auto industry found most attractive in a potential employee.[18]

A newcomer's background largely determined the type of work he or she would secure in Detroit. Auto companies tended to hire American, English, and German men for skilled and semiskilled jobs such as tool and die or machine work, whereas they favored Polish, Hungarian, and Slavic men for unskilled positions, such as assembly work. Auto plants were less likely to hire Jewish and Italian men, more than half of whom turned instead to the service sector, often working as small shop owners or street peddlers. Most automakers steadfastly refused to hire African-American men and women and white women for all but the lowest-paying and least desirable jobs. Black workers were typically segregated into foundry or janitorial jobs, which many white men rejected, and white women were assigned to upholstery or small parts departments, where their "nimble fingers" could be put to best use. There were not many of these jobs, so many black and women workers had no choice but to find work outside the auto industry. African Americans secured jobs as porters, waiters, domestics, and the like, and white women worked in stores, in front offices, or, like Anthonina Tolkacz, within their own homes, which they made into boardinghouses.[19]

Even if a worker were fortunate enough to find a job in an auto plant, he or she was not assured of financial security. The auto manufacturers maintained high wage levels throughout the 1920s, but after the introduction of the annual model changeover early in the same decade, they no longer provided workers with a full year's work. Most autoworkers could expect to lose at least a few weeks' pay—and sometimes much more—in midsummer, while the plants retooled for the next year's production. In 1925, a prosperous year for the industry, for example, a typical autoworker lost six weeks of work, during which he had to live on whatever savings he might have accumulated. On the job, moreover, autoworkers did not enjoy the protection of seniority lists and grievance procedures. The department foreman had the power to lay off, promote, and even fire workers at will, a power some foremen exercised in a brutal and arbitrary manner. "The foreman had the say," one autoworker recalled years later. "If he happened to like you, or if you sucked around him and did him favors—or if you were one of the bastards who worked like hell and turned out more than production—you might be picked to work a few weeks longer than the next guy."[20]

As they struggled to find or keep work, the newcomers also scrambled to find lodgings. In 1900, Detroit had a very low population density; many of the city's blocks were studded with vacant lots. Most of Detroit's workers therefore could afford their own homes. Skilled workers could even hope to enjoy some of the amenities of middle-class life: new furniture and rugs, fresh wallpaper, a few household appliances. Unskilled workers naturally expected less—a small house on a tiny lot, perhaps—but they nonetheless had the ability to own property, which freed them from at least one burden of dependency. By 1916, though, the demand for housing far outstripped the supply. According to one report, some two hundred carloads of household goods lay unclaimed in the city's railroad yards while their owners searched for a place to live. "Laboring men whose presence is much desired in automobile . . . plants," a magazine explained, "are said to be leaving the city because they can find no place to sleep between shifts."[21]

Many of the workers who came to Detroit were young: in 1920, twenty-five to twenty-nine year old men made up 8 percent of the city's population, almost double the percentage of that age group in the nation as a whole. Many members of this "suitcase brigade," as it was known, had little interest in owning a home in the city; they simply wanted to rent while they worked. Their ability to do so, again, was determined largely by their backgrounds. Eastern and southern European immigrants generally turned to the boardinghouses in their ethnic neighborhoods. Conditions varied widely from neighborhood to neighborhood. Polish and Jewish newcomers, for example, were able to move into established communities, whereas Hungarian and Slavic workers did not enjoy the support of existing neighborhoods when they arrived in Detroit. Many boardinghouses did not have running water, proper ventilation, or other basic amenities. Despite such shortcomings, boardinghouse owners, themselves often workers, tried to crowd as many workers as they could into their small homes. In one case, public health officials found fifty-two boarders living in a twelve-room tenement. That was unusual, but it was not unusual for a boardinghouse to rent the same bed to two workers on different shifts. One factory hand would sleep while the other worked.[22]

No matter how poor conditions became in immigrant

neighborhoods, though, they remained far superior to life in Detroit's growing African-American ghetto. One hundred twenty thousand blacks lived in Detroit by 1930, three hundred times the number in 1900. Barred from rental units in most of Detroit by white realtors and landlords, the vast majority of African Americans crowded into the lower east side's black ghetto. There, they were forced to take whatever lodgings they could find. "Seventy five percent of the Negro homes have so many lodgers that they are really hotels," an African-American activist reported in 1917. "Stables, garages, and cellars have been converted into homes for Negroes. The pool rooms and gambling houses are beginning to charge for the privilege of sleeping on pool-room tables overnight." Many landlords, black and white alike, charged African Americans exorbitant rents while refusing to perform the most basic repairs. The owner of a home on Hastings Street, in the heart of the black ghetto, charged his tenants sixty-five dollars a month, almost double the typical rate in white neighborhoods. Yet when the hot water pipe burst he did not fix it, and when a storm blew out the front window he did not replace it. Little wonder that the tenant's infant daughter died of exposure in the middle of winter. The case was far from unusual: Detroit's black community suffered from an infant mortality rate almost double that of white Detroiters.[23]

To be sure, blue-collar life in Detroit could be extremely difficult. It would be a mistake, however, to portray workers as simply struggling through lives of quiet desperation, victimized by employers, foremen, and landlords. On the contrary, Detroit's working people struggled to re-make the city in their image by building a complex web of social structures through which they could promote their values, ease their sorrows, and share their joys. Throughout the 1910s and 1920s, in other words, the million and a half workers who poured into the city made Detroit into their home.

In general, working-class social life revolved around a number of institutions—the church, the social hall, the saloon, and, increasingly, the movie theater, the ball park, and other popular culture venues. Just as workers' backgrounds determined the jobs they secured and the homes they found, however, so too did their backgrounds determine the particular form of the institutions they built.

Nothing better illustrates the diversity of working-class institutional life than the plethora of churches dotting blue-collar neighborhoods. Detroit's Polish workers typically made the local Catholic church the heart of their communities. In the 1920s alone the Detroit Archdiocese established nine Polish-language parishes. "Every high mass . . . is sung in Polish," a disgruntled non-Pole wrote to the bishop. "When the priest intones the gloria, the choir responds with a Polish hymn. . . . In eight months I have not heard the schedule of masses read once . . . in English." Poles turned to the church for spiritual solace, of course, finding in the ancient rituals the comfort of God and of the homeland they had left behind. They found more than that, though: the parish also served as a social center—its altar societies, sodalities, and dances offering workers a chance to meet, gossip, celebrate, and mourn—and as an educational center. When Simon and Anthonina Tolkacz's children were of school age, they were sent to Immaculate Conception's grade school, where they could be instructed in the faith—and in Polish.[24]

Detroit's Jewish workers likewise built their life around the synagogue. In the nineteenth century, the city's Jews—most of German descent—built a vibrant Reform community. The Russian Jews who arrived in Detroit in the early twentieth century, however, found such Americanized services far too distant from their experience. They therefore established a series of small Orthodox synagogues, where the devout could pray, study, and socialize in the tradition of their fathers. "The mood of such synagogues was intense and individualistic," one scholar has recently written. "Prayers were said loudly in Hebrew, by the entire congregation, each person at his own speed and in his own tenor of voice as most worshipers swayed back and forth." Congregation Beth David was fairly typical. A small congregation on the lower east side—it offered services from a rented building for its first twenty-two years—it was nevertheless a thriving spiritual and intellectual community, a place where unskilled immigrants could receive personal guidance and Talmudic instruction from a rabbi with impeccable scholarly credentials.[25] Detroit's African-American community—overwhelmingly Protestant—also divided its allegiances. The city's black elite had long associated themselves with St. Matthew's Episcopal Church; the middle class with Bethel African Methodist Episcopal (A.M.E.) and Ebenezer A.M.E.; the working class with Second Baptist and its sister churches. Southern migrants arriving in the 1910s and 1920s generally shied away from the solemn "high church" services of St. Matthew's, which in any case had little interest in adding laborers to the church rolls. Both the A.M.E. and the Baptist churches, on the other hand, embraced the migrants, providing them with familiar religious rituals, critical social services, and

a strong sense of community. Many African-American newcomers nevertheless found the established churches too large or formal, preferring instead the intense religiosity and communalism of small, fundamentalist "storefront" churches. These churches—high and low—quickly became centers of black empowerment, places where the poorest of Detroiters could direct their own affairs, organize their neighborhoods, and thus exert a degree of political power.[26]

Detroit's workers established a broad network of social clubs for many of the same reasons they built churches. A laborer who joined the Masons or the Knights of Pythias, for example, could find fellowship, empowerment, and often a good deal of ritual. Working-class social clubs met other needs as well. For skilled workers they often served as informal hiring halls, where a newcomer to the city could hear of job openings or meet a fellow craftsman who could provide the all-important reference. When tool and die maker Harold Snudsen arrived in Detroit from England in 1923, he immediately joined both the Masons and the Oddfellows Lodge because, his son explained years later, "he thought . . . he could get a job easier through their influence." Eastern and southern European social clubs did not enjoy that kind of influence. They could provide their members with a greater degree of financial security, however. The Hebrew Free Loan Association or the local chapter of the Polish National Alliance, for instance, offered workers the chance to buy health insurance and death benefits for a low monthly fee, as well as low interest mortgages.[27]

Not all working-class institutions had such high goals, of course. Take, for example, the ubiquitous working-class bar. At least until Michigan outlawed the sale of liquor in 1916—and oftentimes after Prohibition began—workers of various back-grounds made the neighborhood tavern a part of their daily routine, stopping for a shot and a beer on the way home from the plant, perhaps, or whiling away the evening standing for rounds. "After work, we went home, ate supper, and met in a bar, usually Premo's on Jefferson Avenue near the car barn," Frank Marquardt explained. "Though a minor, I was tall and never got turned down by the bartender when I put my foot on the brass rail and ordered, `Gimme a beer.'" Bars did much more than serve alcohol; they also provided customers with in-expensive food, newspapers, pool tables, and basic banking services. Although they provided many social services, bars were not inclusive institutions. On the contrary, neighborhood saloons were usually dominated by a single ethnic group. African Americans frequented the bars and speakeasies of the east side's "Paradise Valley," for instance, whereas Hungarian workers filled Delray's numerous taverns.[28]

Together, churches, social clubs, and saloons incorporated Detroit's workers into tight-knit ethnic communities, neighbor-hood pockets where working people could speak their native tongue, meet others from home, and so on. By 1920, though, the workers' social world had begun to widen, as the movies, radio, and other instruments of popular culture slowly eroded the walls of ethnicity. A number of historians have detailed the process: in the 1920s, they say, workers who spoke little English suddenly could hear hours of English-language radio shows; workers who followed Old World traditions could see middle-class American behaviors on the silver screen. The movies and radio did not simply impose a national culture on Detroit's working people; workers also shaped the culture they received in the theater or over the airwaves.[29]

When Detroiters think of pre-1930s movie theaters, they generally envision downtown Detroit's great picture palaces, such as the Fox or the Grand Circus. Most of the city's working people probably did not see many movies in these cavernous, ornate theaters, however; those theaters generally catered to a middle-class audience, not to factory hands and domestic ser-vants. It was much more common for workers to watch films in small neighborhood movie houses, such as the Arcade on Hastings Street, or the Maxine on Mack Avenue. There, sitting in hardback seats, watching an ill-kept screen, workers often became part of the action, particularly in the days before sound. A Chicagoan tells of a scene undoubtedly repeated in Detroit's neighborhood theaters. When older Italian men went to a western movie, he says, "and when the good guys were chasing the bad guys . . . they'd say, `get em, catch em'—out loud in the theater." Many local movie houses also supple-mented their film offerings with amateur nights, when workers could clamber up on stage and try their hand at entertaining their neighbors and friends.[30]

Detroit's working people also helped to shape radio pro-gramming. In the 1920s Detroit's working people, like other Americans, embraced the new technology with a passion, often building their own wirelesses to capture the entertainment and news now flooding the airwaves. Radio executives shaped their schedules accordingly, airing ethnic, religious, and other shows carefully crafted to appeal to working-class listeners. As late as

1936, one Polish-American remembers, it was possible to walk through Detroit's Polish neighborhoods and hear Walcaw Golanski's Polish-language show playing on every radio. And by 1930 Detroit's most popular radio personality was Father Charles Coughlin, the pastor of Royal Oak's Shrine of the Little Flower, who delivered his weekly sermon over WJR, one of the Midwest's most powerful radio stations.[31]

Despite workers' ability to shape popular culture, ethnic differences began to break down in the 1920s as a variety of institutions "Americanized" the city's factory hands and their children. Some of Detroit's institutions explicitly undermined workers' ethnic culture. The Tolkaczs' children were sent to public high schools, for example, where they had no choice but to speak English, a language their parents did not know. Other institutions Americanized workers by accident, rather than design. In the 1920s, for instance, the Detroit Tigers baseball club built a substantial following among the city's workers, in the process giving factory hands of starkly different backgrounds a common topic of conversation, a common vocabulary, and a common experience. In such small ways, the barrier of ethnicity—if not of race—slowly collapsed.[32]

The Great Depression accelerated the changes in Detroit's working-class communities. The economic collapse of the early 1930s devastated Detroit. Unemployment skyrocketed to 50 percent by 1932 as employers cut their payrolls. Many of those who lost their jobs faced the specters of foreclosure, eviction, and hunger. Those Detroiters lucky enough to keep working watched their wages plummet: the typical autoworker earned half as much in 1932 as he had in 1929. Amid the crisis, work-

ing-class Detroiters began to find more and more common ground. Workers of all backgrounds turned to the Democratic party for relief, seeing in the humanitarianism of Mayor Frank Murphy and the grand promises of Franklin Roosevelt hope for a better day. And workers turned to each other, building labor unions that gave them a sense of power and dignity on the shop floor.[33] Unionization, in turn, further weakened the bonds of ethnicity and race, the promise of solidarity eating away at the divisions that had characterized the city earlier in the century.

Even by the late 1930s, though, that process of change was far from complete. Detroit's factories and neighborhoods, churches and social halls remained a patchwork of ethnic and racial groups, each struggling and competing for a share of industrial America's promise. More importantly, Detroit remained a working-class city, its rhythms set by the rhythms of the assembly line, its air darkened by the smoke of the factory furnace, its economy built by the sweat of a million men and women. It is life in that city that *Muddy Boots and Ragged Aprons* explores—the everyday life of ordinary people, in all their glory.

This book explores the everyday life of Detroit workers through photographs taken between 1890 and 1935. Photographs have their limitations as historical sources. In one way, however, they are a perfect pairing with the city of Detroit: the constant technical innovation that turned photography from a rich person's privilege and pursuit to an amateur's enjoyment mirrors the development of automobiles in the city.

From the official birth date of photography in 1839 through the late 1880s, every decade brought with it a new innovation in photography. The decisive step in the popularization of photography occurred in 1888, when George Eastman introduced the Kodak Number 1, the Model T of cameras, aimed at allowing the mass market to take and enjoy photographs. Just as the rapid industrialization of the northeast allowed consumer goods to flow into the market, just as the constant innovation in the process of building automobiles made them more and more affordable, the Kodak Number 1 greatly simplified the photography process. The result was a tremendous expansion in the ranks of amateur photographers.[34]

Technically, taking a photograph was simple: the photographer merely had to uncover the hole for light to enter the camera, guess how many seconds of exposure to give the film, and hope the subject did not move. Some photographers used a magnesium flash to reduce shadows. Deciding what to photograph was not quite as simple. The photos presented here grow out of three traditions in picture making: portraiture, urban photography, and documentary photography.

From 1845 to 1875, photographers presented their subjects in formal and refined images. Portraits were especially formal, just as painters did. With the introduction of the tintype in the 1860s, the middle class began to patronize photographers in larger numbers, requesting portraits of husbands and wives, children, and especially Civil War soldiers. These photographs too were generally formal, but as sitters grew more comfortable in front of the camera and as the number of portrait photog-

raphers expanded, portraiture began to turn away from the excessively formal poses of the earlier period.[35]

The same sort of movement occurred within the genre of urban photography. The early photos of cities, cityscapes, and urban areas embraced the "grand style" of urban photography, presenting monumental buildings, panoramic vistas, centers of industry, and well-tended city parks. The "grand style" was celebratory, showing the city as an ideal; it avoided references to the poor, to the people who worked in centers of industry, to those who maintained the parks. Indeed, many of these photos had few people in them at all. The publication of Jacob Riis's *How the Other Half Lives* in 1890 changed urban photography, shifting the focus squarely onto the plight of the poor and downtrodden. Riis presented numerous pictures of the hidden areas of the city: alleys, taverns, cellars, and tenement apartments populated by menacing immigrants, doleful children, stoic mothers. He artfully composed his pictures to make his audience recognize the injustices being done to workers and the poor, and by so doing to incite his audience to ameliorative action.[36]

Riis had helped to create a third type of photography, the documentary, a genre that soon came to include pictures of street life, everyday activities, unguarded moments, in addition to the pictures intended to rouse audiences to action. The new blending of documentary and urban photography used photography to objectify the city, to display it as a dynamic social environment. In a sense, the camera became a tool for exploring and ordering the city. And as the camera fell into the hands of more and more amateurs, they captured more and more everyday moments. As anyone who has flipped through a family album can attest, photos were taken not only of memorable scenes, but of ordinary scenes as well, which were then re-membered because of the photo.[37]

*Muddy Boots and Ragged Aprons* emerges from all three traditions of photography. Some photos included in the book are portraiture (H2, W1, W17), albeit generally in a relatively informal style. Some urban photography of the "grand style" is included as well (W20, C29). A few of the photos were meant to tug at a viewer's heartstrings (H12). Most of the pictures, however, are representative of urban photography and depict Detroit as a vibrant social environment. The mix of pictures results from the wide range of photographers included in this volume, from the nameless photographers working for the Ford Motor Company to the professional African-American photographer Harvey C. Jackson, from newspaper photographers to amateurs William C. Weber and George Thorne. Between them these photographers captured Detroit working men and women at home, at play, at sleep, at work, travelling to work, cooking, and tending children.

Like any other historical data, photos from another period require examination and analysis. They do not present their own interpretations. We cannot "read" a diplomatic note sent from Great Britain to Germany in April 1939 without general knowledge of relations between the two countries before World War II. Similarly, we cannot "read" a photo showing a boardinghouse room in Detroit in 1914 without general knowledge of the city, its immigrants, and its industry. In fact, our understanding of both would be immeasurably increased by specific background: that the Germans had occupied most of Czechoslovakia in March 1939; that the picture of the boardinghouse had been taken to suit the purposes of an automobile company.

Unfortunately, even with the plethora of coffee-table books on the art of photography, there are few guidelines for the analysis of historical photographs. Some authors say that the historian must understand photographs intuitively; others recommend examining a whole body of work by one photographer to understand the meaning of a single photograph. Authors in many social science fields—especially anthropology and sociology—use photographs to illustrate their texts. Generally, they take the photos they use at face value, not bearing in mind that the method of photography, the presence of the photographer, and the purposes of the photographer may influence the content, framing, and consequent "message" of the picture taken.[38]

In an effort to avoid these oversights, the historian must ask questions of the photo and the photographer. For what purpose was the picture taken? Was the picture posed? Why did the photographer take this picture and not another? Why did the photographer choose to show the subject from this angle? Why did the photographer choose just this moment? What do the contents of the picture tell us? Can we trust the picture? How was the photo used after it was developed? Are there multiple ways of interpreting the photo? Since, in many cases, the photographers of turn-of-the-century Detroit are unknown or dead, we must carefully ask these questions of the picture alone, being ever aware that we do not possess the full context.

This book includes photographs taken for a number of reasons and in a number of venues. Some of the photographs presented here are part of a set of seventy taken by members of the Ford Motor Company's Sociological Department. They were taken to help investigators determine the worthiness of an employee for the five dollar wage; they were also used to instruct other workers in proper hygiene and living conditions.

Other photographs were taken for insurance purposes by the Manning Brothers Company of Detroit. More photos of early-twentieth-century Detroit were found in collections at the Archives of Labor History and Urban Affairs at Wayne State University, the Burton Historical Collection of the Detroit Public Library, the archives of the Archdiocese of Detroit, the archives of the *Detroit News*, the Henry Ford Museum and Greenfield Village, and the Michigan Historical Collections, Bentley Library, the University of Michigan. Most of them have never been published before.

Looking at the photographs presented here, it still may be hard to imagine working-class life in Detroit in the first third of the twentieth century. It may be even harder to see in the photos—often so harsh, so bleak—just how triumphant that life could be. But in the end, *Muddy Boots and Ragged Aprons* is about the victories of the city's working people, black and white, male and female. Those victories could be very great indeed, as one last example attests.

The Tolkacz family is long gone from its house on Sargent Street. Simon spent thirty years on the Dodge Main loading dock, finally retiring in the late 1940s. He died a few years later. Anthonina died in 1968, living to the end in the home her husband built.[39] Their legacy lives on, though. It lives in the auto industry, where their grandson, Joseph, an engineer, now works. And it lives in their family, which still rests upon the love and commitment that Simon and Anthonina pledged in Immaculate Conception more than eighty years ago. There is no greater triumph than that.

# Notes

1. Interview with Joseph Tolkacz, July 1, 1992, St. Clair Shores, Mich. The wedding date is from the marriage license of Simon Tolkacz and Anthonina Sergej, in Joseph Tolkacz's possession.

2. Joseph Tolkacz interview; Daniel Nelson, *Managers and Workers: Origins of the New Factory System in the United States, 1880–1920* (Madison: University of Wisconsin Press, 1975), 24.

3. Joseph Tolkacz interview; *Detroit City Directory* (Detroit: R. L. Polk, 1912).

4. Joseph Tolkacz interview.

5. Mary Beth Norton et al., *A People and a Nation: A History of the United States*, 1st ed. (Boston: Houghton Mifflin, 1982), A-14; James Barnes, *Wealth of the American People: A History of Their Economic Life* (New York: Prentice-Hall, 1949); Douglass North, *Growth and Welfare in the American Past: A New Economic History*, 2nd ed. (Englewood Cliffs, N.J.: Prentice-Hall, 1974), 39–40. The United States' percentage of world manufacturing output surpassed that of Great Britain between 1881 and 1885. The literature on American industrialization is enormous. For a solid overview, see Edward Kirkland, *Industry Comes of Age: Business, Labor, and Public Policy, 1860–1897* (New York: Holt, Rinehart, and Winston, 1961).

6. On industry's need for labor, see David Montgomery, *The Fall of the House of Labor: The Workplace, the State, and American Labor Activism, 1865–1925* (Cambridge: Cambridge University Press, 1987), particularly chapters 1, 2, and 3.

The precise number of internal migrants is impossible to determine. See Kirkland, *Industry Comes of Age*, 330–31. Immigration figures are derived from Norton et al., *A People and a Nation*, A-15.

7. There is also vast literature on the "new" immigration of the late nineteenth century. For an excellent overview, see John Bodnar, *The Transplanted: A History of Immigrants in Urban America* (Bloomington: Indiana University Press, 1985). John Higham, *Strangers in the Land: Patterns of American Nativism* (New Brunswick, N.J.: Rutgers University Press, 1955), discusses the reaction of native-born Americans to the immigrants. Statistics on the immigrant population of Chicago and New York are drawn from U.S. Census Bureau, *Twelfth Census of the United States, 1900*, vol. 1 (Washington, DC: U.S. Census Office, 1901), lxix. Sienkiewicz, an eventual Nobel laureate, is quoted in Salvatore J. LaGumina and Frank J. Cavaioli, *The Ethnic Dimension in American Society* (Boston: Holbrook Press, 1974), 135.

8. On the transformation of Detroit, see Steve Babson, with Ron Alpern, Dave Elsila, and John Revitte, *Working Detroit: The Making of a Union Town* (New York: Adama, 1984), 2–21. Detroit's ranking among American cities is from *Twelfth Census*, cx. The outstanding study of Detroit's social geography is Olivier Zunz, *The Changing Face of Inequality: Urbanization, Industrial Development, and Immigrants in Detroit, 1880–1920* (Chicago: University of Chicago Press, 1982), from which the statistics are drawn. Richard Oestreicher, *Solidarity and Fragmentation: Working People and Class*

*Consciousness in Detroit, 1875–1900* (Urbana: University of Illinois Press, 1986) discusses nineteenth-century Detroit from a working-class perspective.

9. The booster's comments can be found in Paul Leake, *History of Detroit: A Chronicle of Its Progress, Its Institutions, and the People of the Fair City of the Straits*, vol. 1 (Chicago: Lewis Publishing, 1912), 215. Zunz, *Changing Face*, 94–104, discusses Detroit's industry in the late nineteenth century. Also see Oestreicher, *Solidarity and Fragmentation*.

10. Keith Sward, *The Legend of Henry Ford* (New York: Rinehart, 1948), 7; Joyce Shaw Peterson, *American Automobile Workers, 1900–1933* (Albany: State University of New York Press, 1987), 4; Sidney Fine, *The Automobile under the Blue Eagle: Labor, Management, and the Automobile Manufacturing Code* (Ann Arbor: University of Michigan Press, 1963), 1; Nelson Lichtenstein, "Introduction: The American Automobile Industry and Its Workers," in Lichtenstein and Stephen Meyer, eds., *On the Line: Essays in the History of Auto Work* (Urbana: University of Illinois Press, 1989), 1.

11. U.S. Bureau of the Census, *Fifteenth Census of the United States, 1930*, vol. 3 (Washington, D.C.: Government Printing Office, 1937); Zunz, *Changing Face*, 286; U.S. Department of Commerce, *Statistical Abstract of the United States, 1933* (Washington, DC: Government Printing Office, 1933), 724.

12. Zunz, *Changing Face*, 292–309, details the location of automobile plants. Ford's first plant was on Mack Avenue, on the city's east side. On the move to Highland Park, see Sward, *Legend of Henry Ford*, 22, 33. The statistics on the move to the Rouge are from David L. Lewis, *The Public Image of Henry Ford: An American Folk Hero and His Company* (Detroit: Wayne State University Press, 1976), 161. A fascinating study of work life at the Rouge is Nelson Lichtenstein, "Life at the Rouge: A Cycle of Workers' Control," in Charles Stephenson and Robert Asher, eds., *Life and Labor: Dimensions of American Working Class History* (Albany: State University of New York Press, 1986), 237–59.

13. On the Ford system of mass production, see Stephen Meyer III, *The Five Dollar Day: Labor Management and Social Control in the Ford Motor Company, 1908–1921* (Albany: State University of New York Press, 1981), especially chapters 1 and 2. Peterson, *American Automobile Workers*, gives the story a human face.

14. Meyer, *Five Dollar Day*, 40–41, 83. By comparison, the much less automated Packard plant had a turnover rate of 200 percent.

15. Meyer, *Five Dollar Day*, chapters 6 and 7.

16. Meyer, *Five Dollar Day*, chapters 5, 6, and 7; Lichtenstein, in *On the Line*, 1–2.

17. Zunz, *Changing Face*, 288; August Meier and Elliot Rudwick, *Black Detroit and*

*the Rise of the UAW* (New York: Oxford University Press, 1979), 5–8; Steve Babson, *Building the Union: Skilled Workers and Anglo-Gaelic Immigrants in the Rise.*

18. Frank Marquardt, *An Auto Worker's Journal: The UAW from Crusade to One-Party Union* (University Park: Pennsylvania State University Press, 1975), 7–11.

19. On the auto companies' hiring patterns, see Zunz, *Changing Face*, 332–42. A number of studies explore racial segregation in the plants. See, for example, Meier and Rudwick, *Black Detroit and the Rise of the UAW*, especially chapter 1; and Lloyd Bailer, "Negro Labor in the Automobile Industry" (Ph.D. diss., University of Michigan, 1943), Nancy F. Gabin, *Feminism in the Labor Movement: Women and the United Automobile Workers, 1935–1975* (Ithaca, N.Y.: Cornell University Press, 1990), chapter 1; and Ruth Milkman, *Gender at Work: The Dynamics of Job Segregation by Sex during World War II* (Urbana: University of Illinois Press, 1987) examine the sexual division of labor in auto manufacturing.

20. Allan Nevins and Frank Ernest Hill, *Ford: Expansion and Challenge, 1915–1933* (New York: Charles Scribner's Sons, 1957), 419–21; quoted in Fine, *Blue Eagle*, 15.

21. Zunz, *Changing Face*, chapter 6; John Ihlder, "Booming Detroit," *Survey* (July 29, 1916), 449.

22. Zunz, *Changing Face*, 289, 388–93; Myron Adams, "The Housing Awakening: A City Awake—Detroit," *Survey* (August 5, 1911), 669.

23. There is no single study of Detroit's black ghetto. For information on Detroit's African-American community prior to the massive movement of blacks from south to north known as the Great Migration, see David M. Katzman, *Before the Ghetto: Black Detroit in the Nineteenth Century* (Urbana: University of Illinois Press, 1973). The information in this paragraph is drawn from Zunz, *Changing Face*, chapter 14.

24. Leslie Woodcock Tentler, *Seasons of Grace: A History of the Catholic Archdiocese of Detroit* (Detroit: Wayne State University Press, 1990), 244, 308, 423. It would be a serious mistake to portray Detroit's Poles as single-mindedly devoted to Roman Catholicism, however. In fact, the city's Polish community experienced a number of internal divisions over religion. See, for example, Lawrence Orton, *Polish Detroit and the Kolasinski Affair* (Detroit: Wayne State University Press, 1981) and Leslie Woodcock Tentler, "Who Is the Church? Conflict in a Polish Immigrant Parish in Late Nineteenth Century Detroit," *Comparative Studies in Society and History* 25 (1983): 241–76.

25. Sidney Bolkosky, *Harmony and Dissonance: Voices of Jewish Identity in Detroit, 1914–1967* (Detroit: Wayne State University Press, 1991), chapter 1.

26. Katzman, *Before the Ghetto*, 136–46.

27. For details on ethnic mutual aid associations, see Bodnar, *Transplanted*, 120–30.

and Lizabeth Cohen, Making a New Deal: Industrial Workers in Chicago, 1919–1939 (Cambridge: Cambridge University Press, 1990), 64–83. African-American fraternals are discussed in Katzman, Before the Ghetto, 147–57; Babson, Building the Union, 85–92, has an excellent discussion of fraternal organizations for skilled workers; Bolkosky, Harmony and Dissonance, 26, discusses Jewish self-help organizations; and Zunz, Changing Face, 192, mentions Polish organizations.

28. Two very different, but equally valuable, discussions of the working-class saloon are Roy Rosenzweig, Eight Hours for What We Will: Workers and Leisure in an Industrial City 1870–1920 (Cambridge: Cambridge University Press, 1983), chapters 2 and 4, and Verlyn Klinkenborg, The Last Fine Time (New York: Vintage, 1990). Babson, Working Detroit, 24–25; Marquardt, Auto Worker's Journal, 12.

29. On the integrative power of mass culture, see, for example, Stuart Ewen, Captains of Consciousness: Advertising and the Social Roots of the Consumer Culture (New York: McGraw-Hill, 1976); and Richard Wightman Fox and T. J. Jackson Lears, eds., The Culture of Consumption (New York: Pantheon, 1983). For an excellent discussion of the working-class role in shaping popular culture, see Cohen, Making a New Deal, chapter 3.

30. Detroit News, July 16, 1920; Cohen, Making a New Deal, 123; Rosenzweig, Eight Hours for What We Will, 201–8.

31. Detroit was an excellent city for radio enthusiasts. Station WWJ was the nation's first regularly broadcasting radio station. George Stark, City of Destiny: The Story of Detroit (Detroit: Arnold Powers, 1943), 484–86. Margaret Collingwood Nowak, Two Who Were There: A Biography of Stanley Nowak (Detroit: Wayne State University Press, 1989), 78; Alan Brinkley, Voices of Protest: Huey Long, Father Coughlin and the Great Depression (New York: Vintage, 1983), 91–92.

32. David Tyack, The One Best System: A History of American Urban Education (Cambridge: Harvard University Press, 1974), 229–55; Joseph Tolkacz interview; Steven Riess, City Games: The Evolution of American Urban Society and the Rise of Sports (Urbana: University of Illinois Press, 1989).

33. Babson et al., Working Detroit, 52–60.

34. Photography Rediscovered: American Photographs, 1900–1930, essay by David Travis (New York: Whitney Museum of Modern Art, 1979), 13; Peninah R. Petruck, The Camera Viewed: Writings on Twentieth-Century Photography (New York: Dutton, 1979).

35. Kenneth Finkel, Nineteenth Century Photography in Philadelphia (New York: Dover, 1908), x; William Welling, Collectors Guide to Nineteenth-Century Photographs (New York: Macmillan, 1976).

36. Peter B. Hales, Silver Cities: The Photography of American Urbanization, 1839–1915 (Philadelphia: Temple University Press, 1984), chapters 2, 4, 5; Alan Trachtenberg, Reading American Photographs: Images as History; Mathew Brady to Walker Evans (New York: Hill and Wang, 1989), chapters 1, 4; Jacob Riis, How the Other Half Lives: Studies among the Tenements of New York (1890; rpt. New York: Sagamore Press, 1957).

37. Warren Susman, Preface to Michael Lesy, Bearing Witness: A Photographic Chronicle of American Life, 1860–1945 (New York: Pantheon, 1982), i.

38. Robert M. Levine, "Semiotics for the Historian: Photographers as Cultural Messengers," Reviews in American History 13 (1985), 382.

39. Joseph Tolkacz interview.

# Home

Sorting through boxes full of Ford Motor Company papers at a warehouse in a Detroit suburb several years ago, we came across an old, tattered, leather-bound album containing some seventy remarkable pictures. Black-and-white photos, eight inches by ten, they told a story of the time when Detroit was a booming city, when Detroit's industries drew workers like a magnet, when eastern and southern Europeans, as well as African Americans from the South, poured into the city by the thousands, when every city block saw new construction.

Piecing together the history of the photo album, we realized what an important story it had to tell. In 1914, Henry Ford, in an attempt to cut down on the high labor turnover rate at his factories, offered workers a wage of five dollars a day. Ford workers had to qualify for the wage, however. They should be clean, be free of vices like gambling or drinking, be thrifty, and show signs of becoming good American citizens. Ford had his company's "Sociological Department" investi-

gate the laborers to determine their worthiness for the higher wage. Part of that investigation took the form of photographs of workers' dwellings—these were the photos collected in the album we had found.

In addition to deciding individual cases, the Sociological Department used these photos to teach their employees how to qualify for the five dollar day. In a booklet titled *Helpful Hints and Advice to Employes*, Ford workers could read about "proper" living conditions, the evils of boardinghouses, the importance of fresh air for children, the vices they should avoid, and so forth. Some of these photos were published in that pamphlet, but most of the others have never been published.

When Simon and Anthonina Tolkacz were first married, they lived in rented rooms above a saloon. Although we have no photographs of their first home, we can easily imagine its cramped quarters and lack of privacy. Many of the photos of boardinghouses collected here emphasize their crowded and

*H1 Bedroom of 941 Russell Street*

unsanitary nature. Still, the Tolkaczs were able to save money and build their own home on Sargent Street. Much like the house in photograph H4, this small structure presented a neat face to the world. Simon Tolkacz built the house not far from his work at the Dodge Main factory.

In Detroit, it was not unusual for workers to live a considerable distance from their places of employment. Unlike many major industrial centers, Detroit did not have rows of workers' cottages standing near factory gates. The streetcar system, high labor turnover, and dispersion of plants throughout the city combined to allow workers to live far from the big factories. The worker whose home is shown in photo H7, for example, crossed half the city to get to work each day.

Here, then, are the homes of Detroit. Imagine, as you examine the photos, families gathering around the kitchen tables, weary second-shift men sleeping in the beds during the day, women doing laundry over the washtubs, and children playing in the backyards of these houses.

We begin this section with a consideration of the questions posed by these pictures of workers' homes. Next, we turn to contrasts between older and newer houses, more derelict and more comfortable homes. We take a tour, moving from room to room. The next few photos explore poorer homes in some detail. These are followed by photos focusing on the home as a site of economic production, finishing with pictures showing the boardinghouses that dominated many sections of Detroit.

## Couple on steps

The quiet confidence on the man's face seems to be a reflection on his achievements—supporting his family, providing a good home on a quiet street, holding down a job. The woman holding her sleeping infant (or newborn grandchild?) also is at peace with herself. She may be wearing a domestic servant's uniform, and it is clear that the shoes she wears are practical, not stylish. The questions we can't answer are endless: Is this a single-family or two-family residence (two mailboxes but one doorbell)? Do they rent or own? Is the car parked on the street theirs? Are those carpenter's marks on the step, implying that this is a new house? Did the couple move north during the Great Migration, or have they long been Detroit residents? With no more information than the photographer's name, this couple—their identity and their history—will remain a mystery.

## 793 Russell Street, front view

This older wooden frame house had as one of its distinguishing features a lightning rod. This measure seems wise, given the roof's wooden shingles and the lack of tall buildings or trees nearby. This photo was taken after the introduction of automobiles. But the presence of horse manure and dearth of cars in the street leave the impression that the picture is from the pre-auto era.

Russell Street ran north and south, parallel to John R, north of Highland Park, far from the city center. Even though it was located near the Ford factory in Highland Park, it had a very low population density in 1920. When the area was annexed by the city of Detroit, the residents approved the association with the city, attracted by the city services Detroit could provide, including sewers, sidewalks, and electric lighting, not to mention stops along the streetcar lines. Note that this house does not appear to be linked by wires to any electrical lines—presumably it still has gas lighting

H3

## 23 Elsa Street

Thomas Weich* was born in Wisconsin in 1869. His parents, Joseph and Sadie (we know Sadie was born in 1843), had immigrated to the United States from Germany the year before and had seven children. In 1914, when this picture was taken, Thomas Weich, his wife Louisa (whose parents were born in the United States) and his widowed mother lived together here, at 23 Elsa Street. In the 1910 census, Thomas listed his trade as assembler in the auto magneto industry (see also photo W3). In the city directory in the years following, he is listed variously as a machinist, an autoworker, and a foreman at the Ford Motor Company.

In 1915, Weich moved to Belvedere Avenue, on the city's east side, near the Dodge Main plant. Two years later he and Paul Schaeffler, a clerk in a men's furnishings store, opened their own men's clothing store on Mack Avenue, one of the east side's main thoroughfares. Weich died in 1924 or 1925, in his fifties, and his wife took over his interest in the store. Thomas's brother Joseph moved in with Louisa shortly after Thomas died; Joseph worked as an assembler in the auto industry.

435.

## 23 Elsa Street

This picture shows the kitchen of Thomas Weich's house at 23 Elsa Street. The Ford Motor Company's Helpful Hints and Advice—a pamphlet given to factory hands—held up the kitchen as a model of clean and sanitary housekeeping. "Employees should use plenty of soap and water in the home, and upon their children, bathing frequently," the booklet lectured the workers. "Nothing makes for right living and health so much as cleanliness. Notice that the most advanced people are the cleanest" (p. 13).

The kitchen was up-to-date: it had fashionable wallpaper, the latest model stove, a hot water heater, running water, and gas light. The furnishings tell us a little about the occupants: the spittoon and clothesline (running from the right corner to the door) speak of the man and woman who used the kitchen, as do the spice box, calendar, and picture of a young girl on the door. The photographer did not capture the kitchen at its cleanest, however—note the dishes in the sink.

## 684 Antoine Street, kitchen

The kitchen of 684 Antoine shows many signs of its makeshift nature. The counter next to the sink is made of rough-hewn boards. The spoons and cup hang from nails in the wood. The shelf above the sink hangs from wires fixed to nails in the wall (one of which has split the plaster). The silverware stands in one of the mugs on the shelf, indicating the lack of cupboards or drawers.

The Detroit City Directory for 1914 lists three men living at this address. These men included an eastern European autoworker and a tailor of German-Jewish extraction. Finally, Joseph Ebkin ran a produce business from the same address. One of these men may have had a family and children who used the small chair to reach the kitchen counter.

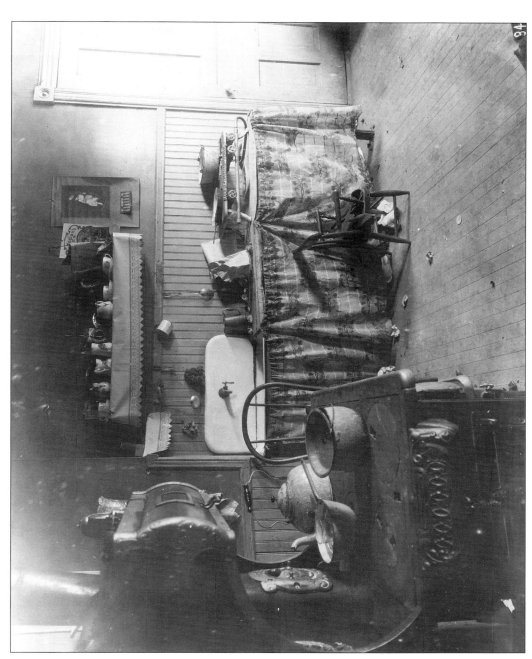

## 159 Buena Vista East, bathroom

Charles Hargraves* could take a streetcar every morning from his home on Buena Vista East to Ford's Highland Park plant. East on Davison, then north on Woodward, and a few minutes later he'd be standing in front of the gate, showing his badge. As a carpenter—a skilled tradesman—and a long-term employee, Hargraves had the ability to save money for the down payment on a home and to furnish it nicely. He must have congratulated himself on his good fortune every morning as he shaved in front of the bathroom mirror pictured here.

Hargraves and his home so embodied management's ideal for its workers that this photo was used as an example to other employees. The room was clean, the Ford Sociological Department pointed out, and the bathtub was certainly used for its intended purpose (unlike tubs placed in kitchens and filled with pots and pans). The potty chair indicates Hargraves had a young child; the room's cleanliness implies Hargraves's wife did not work outside the home. For all these signs of luxury, however, it seems that the family needed extra income: according to the City Directory, Hargraves took in at least one boarder.

## 357 Woodbridge, backyard

*Although the Detroit City Directory listed 357 Woodbridge as a vacant house in 1914, Ford Sociological Department investigators listed eight workers as residents when they took this photo that same winter. Five of the Ford workers, hired between April and July 1913, carried Middle Eastern names. Three of these had very similar last names, but it is not at all clear if they were related. Detroit is currently a center of Middle Eastern immigrant settlement in the United States, but in 1910, they made up only a very small percent of the city's population: there were 417 Middle Easterners in Detroit that year; in 1930, the population had increased to 5,520.*

*The water pump in the yard may have been the only running water for the house. If so, the shed to the left is very likely a privy. The stove inside the house burned the coal stored here in the yard. The residents also used the yard for garbage disposal, washing and drying clothes (note the wash basins on the right and the clothesline on the left), and washing themselves (note the soap dish attached to the third step).*

## 1611 Woodward, living room

Did David N. Harrison,* a mere time clerk at Ford, have the financial wherewithal to decorate his home this way? Or was it the widow Margaret Cummer, with whom Harrison boarded, who displayed these elements of middle-class taste? Apartment number 5 of the Sargossa Apartments on Woodward Avenue had hardwood floors, a gas fire, and electric lights. The residents had a taste for music, heavy Victorian furniture, lace doilies, Oriental rugs, and knickknacks. Note also the family portrait hanging near the corner.

Harrison's Anglo surname is one clue to his identity. Most of the middle ranks of Ford employees—not the shop floor workers or foremen—were native-born Americans. Together with the skilled craftsmen, they often looked down on the eastern European immigrants flooding the city in search of industrial work. As a time clerk, Harrison marked workers' time cards and helped coordinate shifts.

## 27 19th Street, bedroom

*It seems likely that 27 19th Street housed more than just the four Ford workers listed for the residence in the City Directory. Just west of the city center, the area supported a food factory, a fuel factory, a brick manufacturer, various machine shops, a stove works, and stood close to the Michigan Central Railroad. The Studebaker Corporation, Timken Detroit Axle Company, and the city gas company were all located within a half-mile. Workers from any of these enterprises may have boarded here as well.*

*Although two of the residents of the house were carpenters, neither had the time or inclination, it seems (or perhaps the money), to repair the walls of the rooms pictured here. The yard (see photo H12) and walls of the house display a similar state of disrepair:*

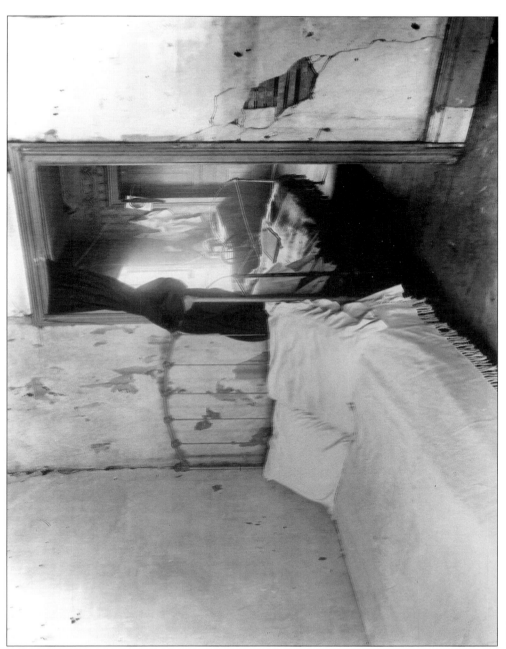

H10

## 27 19th Street, kitchen

This kitchen, with its sloping ceiling, bricked-in fireplace, and peeling wallpaper, tells much about the workers who used it. Worldly possessions and a nicely appointed kitchen were obviously not their highest priorities. The scattered alcohol bottles and matches on the table demonstrate (as some of the better off of the period would put it) ample instances of workers' sins. The room also functioned as the food-preparation area, as the ladles, pots, colander, and milk bottles show. The residents added a few touches of decoration as well, from the framed print on the far wall and the calendars over the mantel to the clock on the mantelpiece. The placement of the chairs, however, suggests that the workers living in the house did not eat their meals together. Close quarters, it seemed, did not necessarily result in camaraderie.

418

## 27 19th Street, backyard

*This photo could have been taken to illustrate the description of unsanitary yards found in Ford's Helpful Hints booklet. These children do not have what the company assured them they needed: open ground and a space for play.*

*The photo was taken between January and March 1914: the snow attests to the season. The yard itself contains a woodpile, an outhouse (behind the woodpile), a clothesline, a washtub, and two warmly clad—though mittenless—children. Note also the pigeon coops: one on a post, one beneath the eaves, and two near the chimney. Pigeon racing was a favorite sport of many immigrants.*

H12

## 446 Frederick, bedroom

A sheetless bed, a doorless room. A makeshift window shade. One shirt hanging on the peg. Newspaper stuffed in the window. Walls that need replastering. We have nothing beyond the names of the Ford workers who shared this bedroom, Abdul Amondi* and Dom Poccia,* both hired at Ford in 1913. The poverty of their surroundings make a cruel mockery of the advertisement in the newspaper for "A splendid mission set"—heavy, dark, substantial furniture.

Ford's Sociological Department members might have viewed the photo in either of two ways. Despite their unprepossessing surroundings, these men keep their living quarters clean and show no signs of reckless spending or such bad habits as drinking alcohol. They thus deserve the chance to earn five dollars a day. Conversely, these two workers, the Sociological Department may have reasoned, chose unhealthy living arrangements, accepted overcrowding, and show no signs of settling permanently in the city, let alone the country. Five dollars a day for Amondi and Poccia would be money foolishly spent.

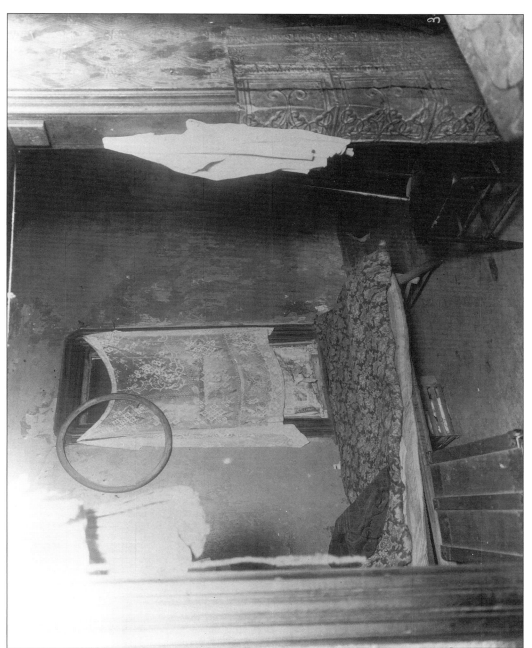

## 441 Frederick

Detroit had a relatively low population density in 1900. Many city blocks contained only a few homes, separated from each other by empty lots. The massive influx of workers in the next two decades forced the city to grow outward, upward, and fill in its vacant areas. Builders and workers built homes wherever they could: between 1916 and 1919 alone, Detroiters constructed more than fifty thousand new buildings. In the process, they pushed the city's population density to levels comparable to that of New York City. By 1920, most Detroit workers lived cheek by jowl with their neighbors in drab, crowded neighborhoods. This block of Frederick Street is typical of the working-class neighborhoods of industrializing Detroit. Note the jumble of buildings in the rear of the photo and the proximity of the two homes in the foreground. Did the residents in the home on the right board up the window to give themselves a modicum of privacy, or were they simply too busy or too poor to replace a broken window?

It is not clear who owned or lived at the house in the center of the photo. The home seems to have been built for more than one family, and at least one of the residents probably worked for the Ford Motor Company. Perhaps he worked the night shift and drew the curtains in the upstairs window so that he could get some sleep. If so, imagine him trudging out the door in mid-afternoon, his cap pulled down low to protect himself from the cold, the porch boards creaking beneath his work boots, the frozen mud crunching as he walked down the street to catch the streetcar to Highland Park.

## Women making fruit jellies

*Workers' homes were also centers of work themselves. Housework could be backbreaking work. These women are making fruit jellies by hand, a process that entails picking or buying the fruit, washing and pitting it, removing stems, cooking the fruit slowly in water until it is very soft, then straining the cooked fruit through cheesecloth or flannel. One 1916 cookbook recommended suspending the bag of cheesecloth over a bowl and letting it drip overnight. The next morning, the juice would be quickly cooked with sugar, as overcooking could ruin the jelly. Finally, the jelly is poured into smaller jars sealed with melted paraffin. Jelly making, another contemporary guide to housewives maintained, is best done on a dry, clear day, so that the sugar will not absorb much moisture. Such preserving work helped farm families get through the winter; in the city, it reduced grocery bills throughout the year.*

*Other women's work—laundry, cooking, shopping, sewing, mending, and cleaning—was also arduous. Beating and shaking rugs in the absence of vacuums; fetching water in the absence of city-laid water pipes; feeding a coal stove in the absence of gas or electricity; wringing, hanging, and ironing clothes in the absence of washing and drying machines made the day an endless series of tasks just to keep the household functioning and the family clad and fed.*

## Polish women en route to the Pingree potato patches

As late as the early 1940s, parts of Detroit remained rural. A Detroiter remembered that when she was young her neighborhood around 23rd Street still had dairies and small farms. "Where we lived," she stated, "we raised chickens in our backyard. We had a full garden in the yard. All the fruit trees had fruit" (quoted in Moon, p. 220).

In an effort to counter the effects of the economic depression that began in 1893, Mayor Hazen S. Pingree proposed that the city's vacant lots be cultivated by Detroit's unfortunate. Families on public relief were given half-acre lots they could cultivate year-round. By 1896, the cash value of the produce grown on these lots exceeded the amount given by the city as poor relief.

These Polish women, photographed heading toward the potato patches, were probably familiar with such farm work. First-generation immigrant women in Detroit varied in their participation in the labor force. In Italian and Bulgarian families, generally, men were the sole breadwinners, while Finnish and Hungarian women were more likely to seek wage work outside the home. Some of these women worked in the fields, but many more worked in cigar factories, sewing rooms in clothing stores, and at sewing machines in upholstery departments of auto manufacturers.

## 440 Kirby, backyard

Is the woman peering out of the second-story window the keeper of this boardinghouse on Kirby Street? Thirteen Ford workers, and who knows how many other laborers, resided here in 1914. The house was well positioned to take advantage of the multitude of new workers in the city. It was a mile south of the Ford Highland Park plant, near the Cadillac factory, and near the Webster-Eisenholer and Mazer-Cressman Cigar companies. In addition to looking after her own family, a boardinghouse keeper cooked for the boarders, cleaned up after them, washed their clothes and bedding, roused the night-shift workers, collected rent, and did all the food shopping. In her few moments of free time, this woman may have turned to the cat perched on the back fence for a little undemanding companionship.

## 110 Manchester

In Ford's 1915 Helpful Hints booklet, this photo is used to illustrate a crowded and unhealthy bedroom. The company preferred that its workers have single-occupancy bedrooms. Ford disapproved of keeping boarders and refused to approve men for the five-dollar day if they "herded" themselves into overcrowded rooming houses (Helpful Hints, p. 13). This photo of 110 Manchester Street, near the Highland Park plant, shows the sleeping quarters of thirty-three men. Most of the men had eastern European first and last names and declared themselves in the city directory to be laborers.

The photo shows what was once probably a living room-dining room area; four beds are visible, but it is clear that the beds were shared—men working the first shift at the plant slept while the second-shift men worked. In fact, two men are seen sleeping in the photo. They hung their clothes above the beds and stuffed their belongings under them. One even hung a reminder of home—a portrait of two women—above his bed.

## 1157 Riopelle, bedroom

Seven beds constitute the main furniture in this room. If each bed slept at least two men, or as many as four—in shifts—then between fourteen and twenty-eight men called this room home. The similarity of the bedsteads, the identical bed coverings and pillows give the impression of a large boardinghouse. The men hang their coats and hats above their beds, their towels at the foot or head of each bed, and coverings on the windows and doors. Presumably, this last was taken as a measure to protect privacy and to block sunlight from workers on the night shift who slept during the day.

Despite the room's spartan appearance, the men who lived there left their mark. The portrait of the Virgin Mary and newspaper tacked to the wall, the glasses on the table, and the cigarette butts under it, speak to the men who passed what little leisure time they had here in this room. Ford Sociological Department members, upon seeing this photo, pointed out the dangers of sleeping with the windows shut—it was a positive danger to health, they maintained, as the residents had to breathe foul air (Helpful Hints, p. 14). The advice undoubtedly went unheeded. This photo, after all, was taken in late winter.

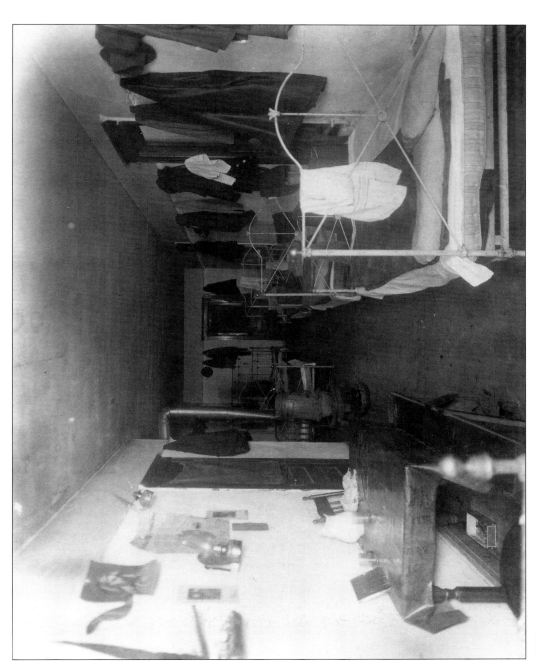

## 118 LaSalle Street, bedroom

*The Ford Sociological Department only listed one worker in relation to this photo, but it seems clear that at least two men slept in this bed. Two hats and two sets of shirts hang upon the wall above the bed. Each man also hung his newspaper on the wall. Under the peaked cap on the right wall hang a newspaper, a tie, and suspenders. Above the other set of pegs rests what looks like a clarinet. One long-term resident of Detroit has remarked that all the old houses lacked closets—hanging possessions above the bed probably seemed the best way to keep things orderly.*

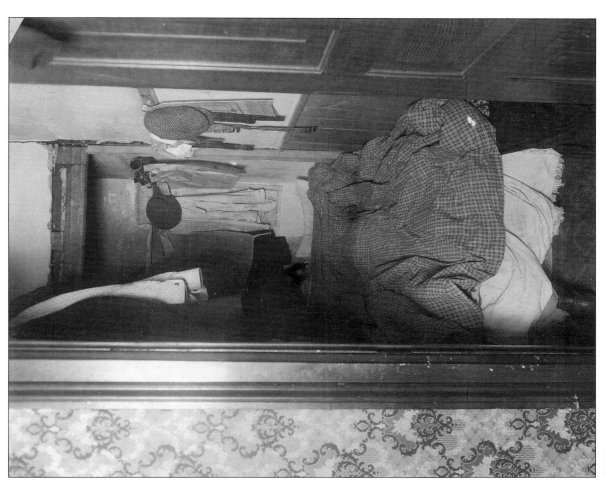

## 778 Woodbridge, bedroom

One of the Ford Sociological Department employees explained the context of this photo. It "shows a room which is used as a bedroom, living room, dining room, kitchen, and is, in fact, a complete home in one room." The company man noted that, in addition to a Ford employee, his wife, and their baby (sleeping at center), the room provided shelter for four boarders. The note from the Sociological Department points out the lack of privacy, ventilation, closets, and chairs. This room was considered unhealthy and a possible breeding ground for tuberculosis.

On a more down-to-earth level, the note accompanying the photo emphasizes the difference between factory hands and the middle class: "The beds do not look comfortable and very few of us would care to try them out. . . . Note how the beds are made up; the quilts are turned back and the sheets exposed. This is done so the quilts will not get so dirty, as the sheets can be washed while the quilts cannot. . . . The baby in its carriage is sound asleep and perfectly happy, although he looks a little uncomfortable." The discomfort, one suspects, was more the observer's than the child's.

H21

## 778 Woodbridge, bedroom

This photo shows more of the room featured in photo H21, which shows the beds and hanging laundry to the right of the coal stove. The photographer in this instance stood in the doorway in an effort to capture as much of the room and the adjoining room as possible. The adjoining room also contains a table and at least one bed—presumably it was used by another set of boarders.

The personal possessions in the closer of the two rooms tell us a bit about Nick Cacciola* and the other boarders. The coal in the bin was for the stove: did the baby's mother guard against her young one popping a piece of coal into his mouth? A man's slippers lie under the table—were these a luxury item for an autoworker? Near the opposite door, a phonograph can be dimly discerned. What sort of music did these men and women enjoy? Finally, do the shoe and the leg attached to it at right belong to Nick Cacciola himself?

## 941 Russell Street, kitchen and bedroom

*This photo brings us full circle. The five Ford employees who boarded in this house probably worked at the nearby Highland Park plant. Two of them are pictured in a bedroom in photo H1.*

*Note the touches that make these rooms home for the workers. The Pet Milk box used for storing possessions under the bed; Brandau's Slippers; the kettle and cookware. Although the surroundings are bleak, Detroit workers strove to rise above dark, cramped rooms and the grind of industrial labor.*

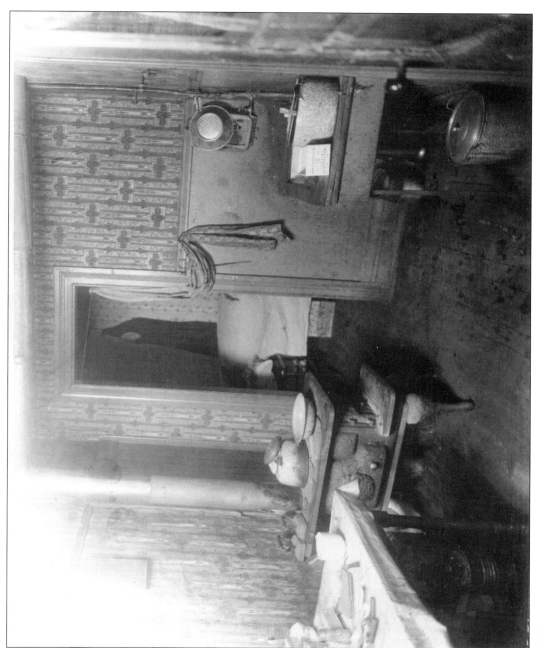

# Work

Think of Detroit, and you think of Ford, Briggs, Fisher, Olds, Cadillac, and Chrysler. You think of assembly lines, automation, and ceaseless toil, of foreign-born and native-born encountering each other on the factory floor. But Detroit at the turn of the century was not just large factories, assembly lines, and soot. It contained thousands of skilled workmen; thousands of women who worked as boardinghouse keepers, laundresses, and factory hands; thousands of men and women who were peddlers and shopkeepers, nurses and housewives, carpenters and casual laborers.

Nor was Detroit's work only ceaseless toil. Construction workers, for example, had several months of little or no employment every year. Autoworkers were hired and fired as the demand for cars fluctuated. Casual laborers were lucky to find work at all, let alone regular employment. And on the job, with the exception of assembly-line workers, most Detroit blue-collar workers' rhythms of work included periods of intense activity and relative quiet. Foundry workers, for example, were a whirlwind of activity as the molten metal was poured from the furnaces, then were warily watchful as they waited for the next heat to be tapped.

Nor was Detroit a city of only factory work. As the city expanded, construction work boomed. Some workers, like Simon Tolkacz, built their own homes. Others helped to build the new houses, shops, and factories that sprang up all over town. Other workers labored on the railroads, in the office buildings, and under the ground. And some labored on the networks that helped Detroit become a trade giant: the railroad and auto tunnels under the Detroit River, and the Ambassador Bridge, linking Detroit and Windsor, Ontario.

Detroit's city limits grew at a steady pace. Between 1900 and 1920, the city tripled in size, reaching 79.6 square miles. Seven years later, it covered 139 square miles. It did so by annexing portions of townships to the east, north, west, and southwest.

New factories arose outside the old city limits: Packard on East Grand Boulevard, Dodge and Briggs in Hamtramck, the Ford River Rouge plant to the southwest. Many plants were erected along rail lines, including Lincoln, the Kelsey Wheel Company, Hudson, Continental, Chalmers, Ford's Highland Park Plant, Paige and Savon. Metalwork factories, industrial goods factories, and parts suppliers also located themselves outside the city center, generally along rail lines. Detroit had no clearly defined factory districts: houses and factories, railroad tracks and apartment houses stood cheek by jowl. Work and home were separated, in many cases, hardly at all.

The pictures gathered in this section come from a variety of sources. They include the archives of the Ford Motor Company and the holdings at the Henry Ford Museum and Greenfield Village. In addition, photos of workers on the line were discovered at the Archives of Labor and Urban Affairs, Wayne State University, and in the Burton Historical Collection of the Detroit Public Library. Some of the more unusual pictures are from Manning Brothers' Photographers. These photos show the factory floor, but they also explore the work of thousands of other Detroiters, from domestics to deliverymen.

Automobile manufacturing starts this section, as befits the industry that dominated the city in the years following 1900. Shifting from primary industries to service industries, we focus next on the small businesses that served the city. The following few photos illustrate how Detroit's institutions dealt with the influx of workers, foreign and native, who flooded into the city. Next, we turn to groups of workers posed in their workplaces. Finally, transportation networks, both within the city and connecting it to the rest of the country, show the avenues through which ore, steel, cars, beer, and fresh fruit and vegetables reached their consumers.

*W1   Ford Motor Company employee, c. 1915*

## Workers assembling wooden autobodies, c. 1905

Prior to the 1910s, auto work was largely skilled work. Craftsmen produced auto parts by hand. Molders and coremakers made metal engine parts, machinists tooled and assembled engine blocks, and carpenters, pictured here, built and assembled auto bodies. An auto's component parts were brought together in a central shop, where assemblers pieced them together.

Steeped in generations of craft pride, skilled workers were fiercely protective of their rights on the job. By tradition, skilled workers determined how they would perform their work and how quickly the work would be completed. Craftsmen also tended to be perfectionists, more concerned about quality than quantity. This workshop reflects the craftsman's cast of mind. The shop is orderly. Coats and hats are hung by each work station, plans and parts are neatly arranged on the shelves along the back wall, and the craftsmen's tools are carefully assembled on the windowsill. Most of the workers stand at rest, staring resolutely into the camera; there is none of the fear or frenzy of assembly-line work here.

Early auto manufacturers found their reliance on craftsmen frustrating and troubling. The leisurely pace of work made it impossible for automakers to mass-produce automobiles, while the skilled workers' autonomy undermined the owners' ability to discipline their workers. These concerns, as much as the demands of the marketplace, led Henry Ford and other automakers to invest heavily in new technology and production techniques that could take the skill out of auto work. The result was the assembly line, which put semiskilled and unskilled workers in the craftsmen's place.

W2

## Ford magneto assembly line, 1913

Technical innovation in the automobile industry went hand-in-hand with technical innovation in the production process. In the very early days of auto manufacturing, individual craftsmen made all or most of a single car. By 1913, Ford was assembling its new Model T on an automated assembly line. Unskilled and semiskilled laborers were put to the same repetitive task day in and day out. The men in this photo assemble magnetos, flywheels to supply current for ignition and lights, which replaced the dry batteries of earlier models. Each man has a single job to do—the first man in the line fixes the bolts on the wheel; the second man adds more material; the fifth and sixth men screw the bolts into place; and so on down the line. The men in the line behind perform similar tasks. The level of mechanization on this assembly line is fairly minimal: while the line is automated, two men are using hand tools to tighten bolts while a third uses a hydraulic tool.

The level of workplace comfort and safety is also minimal at this plant. The first two workers wear aprons, but all the men seem to be lacking any protective gear. The men are bundled against the cold in the factory and have no place to sit down or lean while working on the line. All this for $2.50 a day, twelve hours a day.

## Women in the decorating department of the Jeffery-DeWitt Sparkplug factory, 1912

Compare this photo to any of the shots of assembly-line work. There, parts are stored in graded bins, men stand at their numbered stations, hands always busy. Often a foreman cannot be seen because the assembly line imposes its own discipline. Here, the women sit at long work tables, and they have paused in their activities to stare into the camera. The supervisors are standing over the young workers, posing as well. Parts and materials are stored haphazardly along the wall or at the ends of tables. The tables themselves are positioned near the windows to take advantage of the natural light, even though electric lights are strung overhead. The women seem to be treating the knobs with the substance in the long-handled pot at the end of the table. Their sleeves are rolled up, but, like the men, they do not wear protective clothing.

## Foundry work, n.d.

These men stand at the base of a furnace, tapping it at the optimal moment to fill their ladle with molten iron. The men behind them wait, as their ladle is not yet ready to be filled. The furnace men do not wear any protective gear, despite their proximity to the blinding heat of the burning coal and melting metal. From the furnace, the molten metal will travel in the ladles suspended from the overhead rail to be poured into molds (see photo W6).

White-hot metal and thick clouds of soot were the hallmarks of the foundry. One furnace tender recalled that the heat made all the workers' clothes sticky with dirt and grease within five minutes of starting a shift. Faces were so covered with oil and dust that no skin showed. "We'd walk through on our lunch period to talk to a friend. We couldn't recognize him by his clothes or looks," he remembered. "The men working in his section would tell us where he was or we could tell a friend by his voice" (Denby, p. 30).

When Simon Tolkacz came to Detroit in 1907, he obtained employment in the Ford foundry. The work, he told his children later, was hot and exhausting. His wife agreed. She also worried that the dangers of the job might make her a widow and their children fatherless. Before long, Simon procured much less dangerous work at the Dodge Main factory.

## Ford workers in Highland Park plant pouring molds, November 27, 1914

Ford Motor Company employees pouring molds at the Highland Park plant in 1914. The molten metal was transported from the blast furnace in heavy ladles suspended from the track fixed to the ceiling and pulled along by one man in a three-man unit. Once the metal was in position over a closed mold (open ones are in the foreground), a second man tilted the huge pail to pour steel into the mold. The third man (pictured here with his back to the camera) shoveled sand over the opening and made sure the case was properly closed. The metal gave off steam as it cooled—note the vapors rising from the filled molds behind the men.

Manipulating molten metal was hot, difficult, and dangerous work. A small slip on any man's part could result in injury to all of them, a fact of which they were well aware. They had to pour the hot metal slowly, because pouring too fast caused molds to explode. A foundry worker described the dangers of the job: "The iron would drop on a wet spot and hit the men like a bullet and go into the skin. The man getting hit still had to hold the ladling iron level to keep from burning the other men. They would wait their chance and pick out the balls of iron" (Denby, p. 31). The workers wear gloves and goggles, and stand well away from the hot ladle.

## Early automotive machine shop in a G.M. factory, c. 1910

*The clutter of this General Motors machine shop stands in marked contrast to the order and space of the pre-automated body shop (photo W2). Newcomers to the factory floor were continuously struck by the tremendous noise level. A reporter visiting a Ford machine shop remarked that the "flapping, flying, leather belting," the "rows of writhing machines," the "shrieking, hammering, and clattering," reminded him of "one thing, and that thing was delirium" (quoted in Holli, p. 134).*

*Accidents were common under such conditions. Though the auto industry had a better safety record than most other industries, autoworkers still suffered a variety of injuries on the job. Many were minor; lacerations, contusions, and punctures, for example, were frequent. Others were much more serious. So many machine handlers like those pictured here lost fingers that one commentator called Detroit "the 8-finger city." Ford reported 192 severed fingers at its Highland Park plant in 1916 alone. Mill operators ingested so much dust that they reported "spitting up rust and blood" (Peterson, p. 63). And in the worst auto factory accident of the era, twenty-one paint sprayers at Briggs were killed in April 1927 when ungrounded metal nozzles sparked a fire that raced through the highly flammable lacquers. Workers' clothes, saturated with paint, instantly went up in flames.*

**Workers at milling machines manufacturing parts for the Liberty aircraft engine, Lincoln Motor Car Co., 1918**

*Shortly after the United States entered World War I, military and engineering experts met to discuss the country's aircraft program. Instead of copying British airplanes and components, these men decided that the United States should arrive at its own specifications for military airplanes. Members of the Bureau of Standards, auto manufacturing engineers, and engine experts designed the Liberty Engine in early June 1917. The first ones were manufactured by the end of June. The government placed orders at auto companies and thousands of the 400 horsepower engines were produced at Packard, Ford, Lincoln, Nordyke and Marmon, Willys-Overland, Olds, and General Motors. Here, young men are standing at milling machines at the Lincoln Motor Car Company. By the end of the war, American factories were turning out 150 engines a day.*

*The youth of these workers indicates that they may be apprentices. Machinists stressed the importance of practical training over book learning and wanted their apprentices to become all-around mechanics or machinists, not mere machine tenders. Such a machinist—one of the most skilled trades—had technical knowledge and the ability to direct others. As such, the machinist was valuable in designing specialized machinery such as an aircraft engine.*

## African-American material handler, n.d.

Most auto manufacturers refused to hire African Americans prior to World War I. The wartime labor shortage forced automakers to change their hiring practices, however, and from 1918 onward, the number of African-American autoworkers steadily expanded. Ford, for example, employed only fifty blacks in January 1916; by 1923, the company had five thousand African Americans on its payroll.

World War I did not eliminate the auto industry's discriminatory practices, however. While some auto firms—Ford, Briggs, and Packard, in particular—opened jobs to blacks, others continued to bar African Americans from employment. Those shops that did hire black workers typically relegated them to the lowest paying, most dangerous, or most menial jobs available. More than half of the African Americans employed at the Ford Rouge plant worked in the foundry, and most others labored as janitors, sanders, paint sprayers, or, like the men pictured here, material handlers. Employers obviously cared little about the men relegated to such positions.

Note the workers' makeshift gloves, their only protection from the sharp edges of newly cut castings. Even so, blacks working in the auto industry were seen as "big shots" in the community, as they always had paychecks and earned roughly twice the usual salary of a black man in a service job.

Despite the pervasive discrimination and the difficult working conditions in the auto factories, African Americans from the South poured into Detroit in the 1920s in search of such work. Between 1910 and 1920, while the population of Detroit more than doubled, the population of African Americans in the city increased nearly seven-fold. By the spring of 1920, more than one thousand black migrants arrived in Detroit weekly. A 1920s blues song captured the city's appeal. "I'm goin' to Detroit, get myself a good job," the lyrics rang. "Tried to stay around here with the starvation mob. I'm going to get me a job up there in Mr. Ford's place. Stop these eatless days from starin' me in the face" (quoted in Meier and Rudwick, p.5).

## Women inspecting pistons and valves, Lincoln Motor Car Co., 1918

*When Woodrow Wilson asked Congress for a declaration of war in April 1917, he proposed universal military training, or conscription. Four million men were in uniform by late 1919, many of them married. As white men left their jobs in industry to join the army, employment opportunities opened up for women and African Americans. Still unable to vote, women hoped that the war would allow them to achieve equality with men. Their hopes were dashed, however, as women's employment was limited and brief. About a million women took up war work, but few were "first-time" hires.*

*Most women employed in industrial jobs vacated by men were single girls who moved up from less well-paying jobs. Some were married, helping their families make do while the breadwinners were at the front. Note the older woman seated second from the left. Was her husband "over there"? Some of the men remained in the factories, of course; note the foreman standing at right. The flag hanging in the background was probably put there to remind the women of their relatives in the army and to spur them to work harder, save their wages, and buy war bonds.*

## Ford workers installing piston rings, Ford Rouge, early 1930s

*When the Ford Motor Company perfected the moving assembly line in June 1914, the company's flagship Highland Park plant was considered a marvel of technological innovation. Ten years later, the plant was outmoded, too small to meet ever-expanding demand, too inefficient to take full advantage of the newest production techniques. Ford therefore began shifting the bulk of its production to its new manufacturing complex on the banks of the Rouge River in Dearborn.*

*The Ford Rouge plant was a triumph of integrated production, the greatest factory complex in the world. Sprawled across 1115 acres, the Rouge contained the world's largest foundry, a major steel mill, a paper mill, a body-making plant, and a massive assembly plant. The sheer size of the complex must have overwhelmed workers who, just ten years earlier, had struggled to adjust to Highland Park. The twelve men pictured here assem-*

*bling piston rings account for .00015 percent of the Rouge work-force, which by 1929 numbered seventy-five thousand. The pro-duction process added to workers' sense of powerlessness. The plant was designed so that factory hands never had to leave their work stations—the parts simply came to them. And the shop floor was so crowded with machinery that workers couldn't walk from one part of the plant to another: Anyone wishing to do so had to use the catwalks above the workers, from which this photo was taken.*

*Note also the cleanliness of the plant. "Old Henry Ford wanted his plants clean," Ford worker Walter Rosser remembered, "and so they were kept clean." You could almost eat off the floor, as there were five thousand people in the janitorial division. Every time there was a breakdown on the line, Rosser continued, "instead of being sent home we would assist in cleaning up or paint over and over again" (quoted in Moon, p. 140).*

## Ventura fan

Detroit contained a multitude of service industries, as well as factory-based work. E. Zeigler's bakery in Detroit was typical of many working-class neighborhood institutions. In the days before chain groceries reached most areas, storefront operations comprising a few rooms—bakeries, fish and meat vendors, cigar stores—dominated the main business streets of every neighborhood. Zeigler, it seems clear, baked for the basic needs of his clientele, making breads and rolls, but there is evidence of sweet teeth being catered to, as well—those are eclairs and doughnuts behind the bread; there are muffin tins on the floor.

Although Zeigler's bakery probably served no more than a few hundred customers, the shop was not untouched by outside forces. A national brand of shortening rests on the bread tray. The stove was manufactured in Chicago. In fact, this photo was taken not to document the existence of the bakery to future Zeiglers, but to record the recent installation of a ventilation fan by a sanitary engineer.

## Interior of the Lynn Grocery Co., Lynn and Cameron, March 1916

*When a Detroit housewife walked into the Lynn Grocery Company in 1916 with her list of the week's groceries, she could count on finding canned vegetables, dry goods, and a few specialty goods, such as imported olives and olive oil. The aproned help would bustle around, gathering the groceries for her and weighing out the dry goods. He would ring up her purchases on the modern Keith System cash register. She would set out for home with her groceries, stopping on the way at the butcher's, perhaps, to pick up a bit of meat and some bacon grease in which to fry it. Fresh fruits and vegetables could be bought from peddlers who circled working-class neighborhoods every day.*

## YMCA Americanization efforts

*The concerted effort made by large employers to "Americanize" their workforce started in earnest in Detroit around 1915. Declaring that they wanted to teach citizenship (not to mention good work habits, such as punctuality, obedience, reliability, and respect for authority) to all, the YMCA, the Board of Commerce, and large employers reached out to both the foreign- and the native-born. This classroom, in fact, seems to be dominated by the native-born-African Americans who came to Detroit from the South. The students are not learning English, as the writing on the blackboard demonstrates, but basic business etiquette. It reads:*

Mr. White
Detroit Steel
Detroit, Mich.

Name
Badge #
Address

*Were the men being taught to write letters to employers, or merely learning the name of their own employer?*

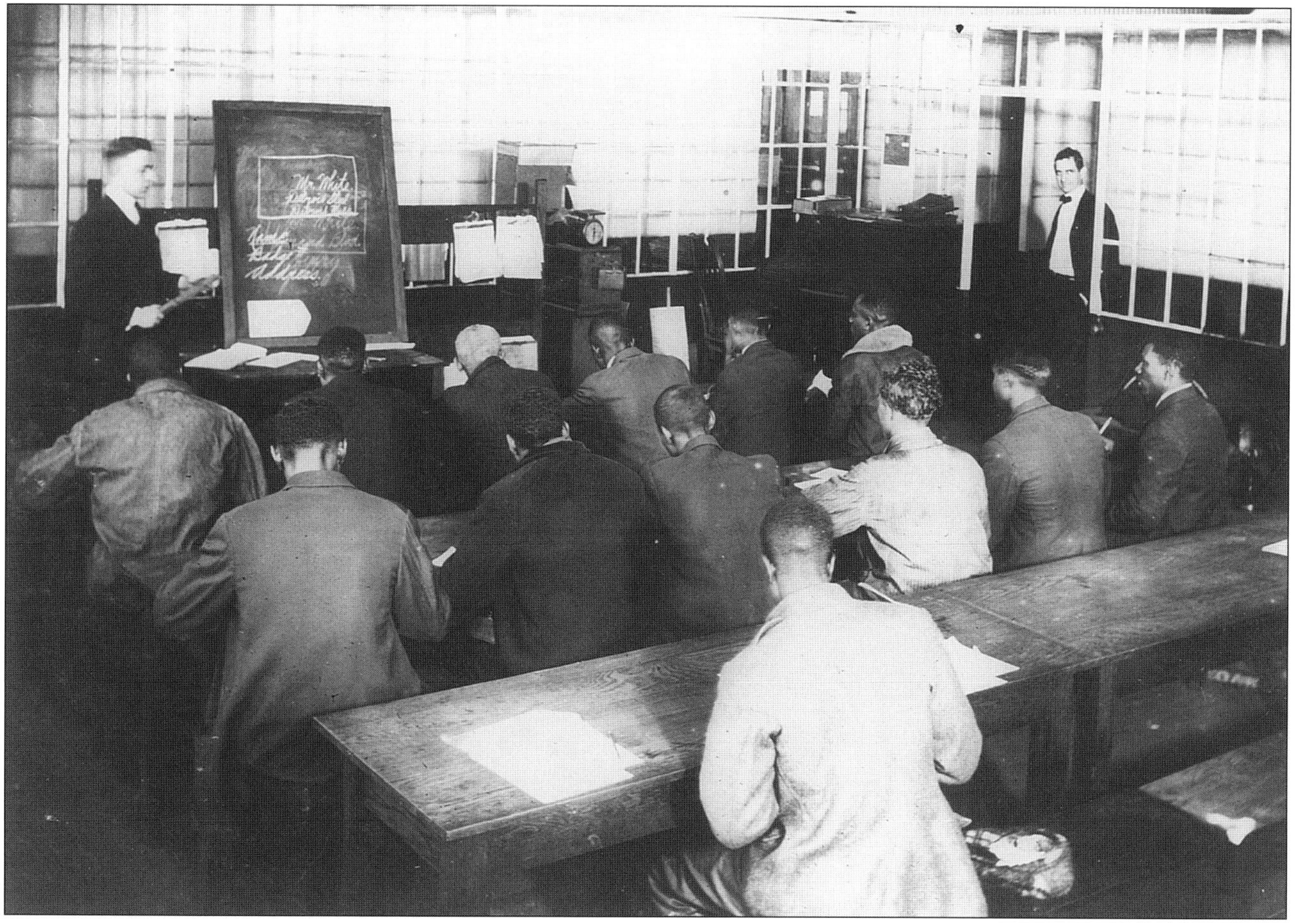

*W14*

## Detroit Shipbuilding Yard, Americanization efforts

In 1915, the Americanization committee of Detroit declared its purpose: "to promote and inculcate in both native and foreign born residents of the metropolitan district including and surrounding the city of Detroit, the principles of American institutions and good citizenship, to the end of encouraging and assisting immigrants to learn the English language, the history, laws and government of the United States, the rights and duties of citizenship; and in becoming intelligent Americans" (quoted in Zunz, p. 313). Composed of the city's large employers, plus attorney Horace Rackham, director of the Ford Sociology Department John R. Lee, and the YMCA general secretary A. G. Studer, the committee organized night school classes in the public schools and in the factories.

Posters were placed in all the factories, urging men to go to school to learn English. "Everyone in Detroit jumped into the campaign with enthusiasm," an observer wrote in 1916. The posters were everywhere, and the message was everywhere. Even department stores had clerks put flyers in "the packages of every customer who looked like a foreigner" (quoted in Holli, p. 138).

The Detroit Shipbuilding company, on the Detroit River at the foot of St. Aubin Street, employed hundreds of men (500 in 1900). As such, it was targeted for the YMCA's program of Americanization. Here, instead of a language class, the men are being taught a song. The national anthem, perhaps? As the event takes place at the factory during a break, the YMCA workers are casting as wide a net as possible, catching both the foreign- and American-born. Many of the men, especially on the fringes of the crowd, are paying little attention to the song, preferring to talk with their friends.

## Stroh Brewery Co. workers holding tools of trade, n.d.

Bernhard Stroh immigrated to the United States in 1848, one of thousands of Germans who escaped the revolution ravaging his homeland. Two years later he opened a small brewery on Detroit's east side. By 1900, the Stroh Brewing Company was one of the city's largest firms, employing 110 men at its Gratiot Avenue plant. Unlike auto manufacturing, Stroh's didn't simplify its production process as it expanded operations. In the early twentieth century, the company still used traditional brewing methods to make the high quality lager favored by working people throughout the city.

Here, a portion of Stroh's skilled hands proudly display the tools of their trade. The four men in the upper left lean on the paddles they use to skim yeast off the brewing beer. A cooper, hammer in his hand, and his aproned crew stand in front of their barrels, which had to be air-tight to preserve the lager as it aged. Several of the men hold tasting cups, which they used to test the beer as it fermented. The dark-faced men in the second row, their shirts stained with soot, are coal-heavers, responsible for maintaining the brewery furnaces. And in the first row are the brewery's elite—brewers and foremen—wearing bowlers and Tyrolean hats, which set them apart even in a plant of proud craftsmen.

## Detroit Police class, 1920

When American cities first began organizing police forces during the nineteenth century, the men (and the police were all men until early in the 1900s) scorned the idea of wearing uniforms. They were not servants, police protested, and would not wear livery. (They also objected to the motto "to serve and to protect.") By the 1920s, the uniform was no longer a badge of shame—the central figures in this photo, the police class instructors, proudly wear their uniforms before the class. (A different style of police uniform can be seen in the photo of the 1901 parade [C15].)

Detroit businessmen had organized a private police force of night watchmen for the downtown district in the 1850s. By the 1860s, however, they realized that private police were not enough. They lobbied for public support of a police force and, on the fifteenth of May, 1865, the first publicly supported police patrolled the city. These policemen patrolled the entire city, but placed an emphasis on watching the business district.

The Common Council of the City of Detroit was selective in its choice of policemen. Police, it decided, had to be Detroit residents of at least two years' standing. They also must speak English; as a result, most Detroit police were American- or Irish-born. Note the similarities among these aspiring policemen: besides their gender, they are united by their youth, their race, their lack of strong ethnic characteristics.

Class of August 1920
Detroit Police Training School

## Dunbar Memorial Hospital, 1930

When the board of trustees visited the Dunbar Memorial Hospital in its new quarters on Brush Street on September 14, 1930, they took the opportunity to have a photo taken. The staff and doctors joined the trustees in front of the hospital. The participants arrayed themselves by rank: the medical director and the superintendent of nurses stood front and center, with the trustees and doctors surrounding them. In the back, nurses and student nurses stood peering out over the wall and between leaves of bushes.

By 1930, the African-American community in Detroit was thriving. Opened in 1918 to train black nurses and doctors and to serve African-American patients, Dunbar Memorial Hospital outgrew its buildings on Frederick Street within ten years. The old hospital had stood at the nucleus of the black neighborhood, across the street from Bethel A.M.E. Church and Charles Diggs

Undertakers. The trustees in 1930 were the well-to-do of the black community. The president, W. C. Osby, was employed as an engineer at the Madison-Lenox Hotel; the first vice-president, Walter Fields, was in insurance; the secretary-treasurer, Charles R. Webb, was a clerk with the U.S. Internal Revenue Service. The other trustees were Walter Dean, Mrs. Anna Green, Mrs. G. M. Humphrey, and Dr. William E. Johnson, a surgeon.

As the Great Depression set in, the hospital began to falter. The number of patients dropped from 2,215 in 1930 to 991 in 1931. The nurses' training school suspended operations in 1931, and all the pupils were transferred to St. Louis Hospital Number 2, in St. Louis, Missouri. The hospital's debts—incurred when building the new hospital—also proved to be a crushing financial burden. The hospital managed to survive, however. Renamed Parkside Hospital, it remained open until 1963.

cal Staff, Trustee Board and Corps of Nurses. Dunbar Memorial Hos

W18

## Domestic servants, c. 1930

In the 1920s and 1930s, most domestic servants worked alone or with one other employee and many worked for two or more families. Having a large group of "help," such as the one pictured here, was a luxury reserved for the rich. Compared to other cities, Detroit recorded a relatively low number of women working as servants, mainly because the city provided other work opportunities—especially in manufacturing—for women. Even so, the employment of a maid, or at the very least a laundress, helped to define the middle class in the 1920s.

Women who went to work as domestics searched for respectable positions, sympathetic employers, clean living quarters (if they lived in), and reasonable hours. A standard workday started before eight a.m., with preparation of breakfast, and proceeded through serving breakfast, washing the dishes, making the beds, scrubbing the bathroom and kitchen, making lunch, dusting, housecleaning, preparing and serving dinner, washing the dishes

and cleaning up after guests departed. Monday brought wash day; Wednesday was reserved for cleaning the silver; Thursday brought housecleaning and window washing; servants cleaned the kitchen thoroughly one day a week; on Saturday, the maid prepared the Sunday dinner. Employers generally gave domestics Thursdays and every other Sunday off (after their regular tasks were complete).

Women who worked as live-in servants often complained about their long hours and loneliness. Taking a room in someone else's house precluded informal socializing with friends. The servants pictured here may have been more fortunate in having many coworkers with whom they could interact. The dullness and monotony of the work reinforced the class tensions between employer and worker. Perhaps that is why the mistress of this house—is it she in the window?—is not standing with her servants for this portrait.

## Michigan Central Railroad tunnel, c. 1900

*Detroit's transportation networks helped the city to expand at the beginning of the industrial era. Construction of the Michigan Central Railroad continued apace in the early 1900s. One can easily detect the signs of ongoing construction in and around the railyard. Is the man in the hat and topcoat bent over his papers directing the work of the railmen on the left? Or is he a civil engineer, checking the layout of the yard against the blueprints?*

*The factories forming the backdrop to the railyard line the Detroit River, facing Canada. It was through Canada that a large proportion of the "old" (Irish, English, and Scots, in particular) immigrants came to Detroit. Trains coming from Canada, like this one, carried freight and passengers who helped to build Detroit in the days before it became an auto manufacturing center. In the south, labor agents sent to recruit workers would run "labor trains" to northern cities. Trains coming from the south and east carried the immigrants who populated the city's plants in its boom years.*

## Streetcar scene, Fort and Clark streets, June 1919

*Although autoworkers were among the most highly paid industrial workers in the nation, most could not afford to buy cars. According to one estimate, only a third of Ford's factory hands owned their own automobiles in 1929. Workers therefore relied on Detroit's extensive network of streetcars, which provided clean and reliable transportation for only three cents a trip.*

*Frank Angelo remembers taking the streetcars in the 1920s. "You'd get on that Baker streetcar, and the odors of the Ford Motor Company workingman were all over the place. I was a bright young kid," he reminisced, "and dressed in my school clothes, and everybody else was in denim, dark clothes, and headed for work at Ford. Everybody just sat silently" (quoted in Moon, p. 40).*

*Nineteen nineteen was a depression year, but when the shifts changed at Timken Axle, the street still buzzed with activity. The young men in boater hats, perhaps front office clerks, stride past the newsboy, who is probably hawking the News or the Times, the city's working-class newspapers. Men in cloth caps—the symbol of working-class status—catch a smoke under the watchful eye of a burly policeman while waiting for the streetcar to arrive (photo a). And as workers, black and white, board the car for the ride home, a second shift laborer, lunch pail in hand, trudges off to the plant (photo b).*

W21b

W21a

## Belle Isle Bridge under construction, March 1920

For all its burdens, factory work at least provided men and women with steady work for most of the year in the 1910s and 1920s. Many other Detroiters worked a succession of odd jobs in the course of a year, often interspersed with days or weeks of unemployment. The ironically termed "casual laborers" swept the city's streets and shovelled the city's snow, dug ditches and laid sewers, the kind of work that required no skill—just a strong back and an extraordinary level of endurance.

Casual laborers found their jobs through personal connections, a brother-in-law who knew a contractor, for instance. Others simply walked the streets in search of work, gathering at a contractor's gate early in the morning, hoping to latch on to a work crew for the day. Casual laborers thus lived a much more precarious existence than many of their fellow working Detroiters.

The men captured in this photo are digging the foundations for the Belle Isle Bridge. Having a paycheck for a few weeks, they might join the better-paid workers of the nearby Morgan Wright Tire Factory for a hot lunch at one of the restaurants on Jefferson Avenue. Once the foundation was laid, however, they would be back on the streets, facing a bleak future.

## Ambassador Bridge

*When it became clear, in the early 1910s, that the railroad tunnel and the ferries were inadequate to meet the demands of commerce between Canada and the United States, plans were drawn up to build a bridge over the Detroit River. To allow Great Lakes vessels to pass under it, the bridge had to be at least 110 feet high at the center. When architects decided that a suspension bridge would be the most appropriate structure for the spot, the contract went to the McClintic-Marshall Company, which had recently finished construction on several suspension bridges on the East Coast. McClintic-Marshall hired subcontractors: the Foundation Company of New York for the main piers and the anchorage substructures; the Keystone State Corporation of Philadelphia for the main span cables, suspenders, and hand rope. The directors made a concerted effort to purchase Canadian materials and services for the Canadian side of the bridge and American materials for the American side. At times, there were more than six hundred workers—Canadians on one side, Americans on the other—on each side of the bridge.*

*After the two anchorages and towers were built, two footbridges were suspended, along with cross-over spans. These allowed workers to hang the cables that would eventually hold the bridge. Here, two workers drag some heavy object across the footbridge. Little do they know that the suspension cables will soon be found to be breaking and in need of replacement; the contractors will be forced to take down the footbridges and the cables and start again with new suspension wires.*

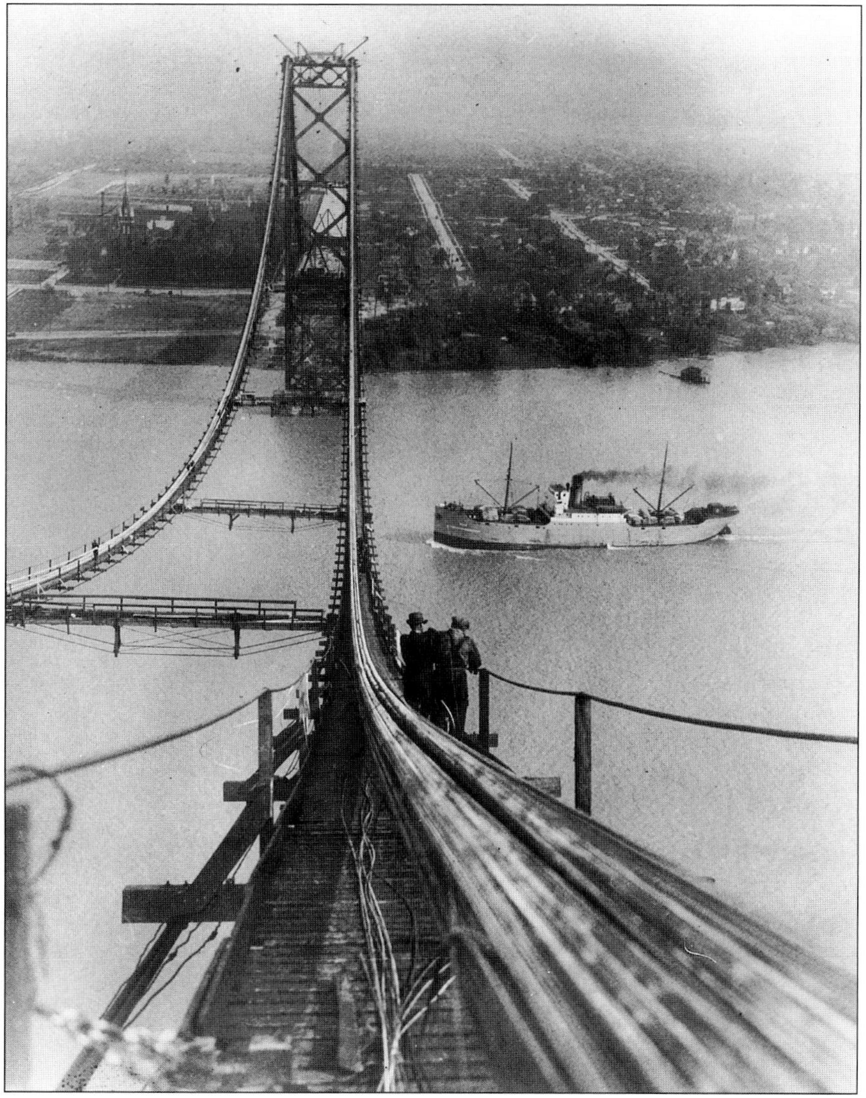

*W23*

## National Tea Company deliverymen, 1905

In 1905, the nine deliverymen of the National Tea Company lined up with their horses and wagons for this portrait. The street is unpaved; horse manure dots the street. The men wear sturdy, mud-spattered boots, ties, topcoats, and bowlers. The horses are thin and bony. In addition to delivering the tea to grocery stores, these men peddled dry goods in the streets, joining the ranks of fruit, vegetable, and dairy vendors who circled Detroit neighborhoods.

The National Tea Company was owned by a Danish man, but it is unlikely that these employees were also Danes. Denmark sent a very small proportion of its American-bound emigrants to Detroit. Most Danes in Michigan settled on farms instead of in the cities. These drivers might have been Italian, as a high proportion of Italian immigrants got their start in delivery businesses.

W24

## Stroh Brewery deliverymen

*Compare this photo to the one of the National Tea Company deliverymen. Instead of horses, the Stroh's deliverymen use horsepower—the internal combustion engine. The street is asphalt; there is no manure to be seen. Companies took advantage of advances in transportation to increase their revenues and widen their distribution of products. Even though the changes wrought by the automobile revolution in Detroit were dramatic, many elements of continuity can be seen as well. The Stroh's truck is structurally very similar to a wagon: the wheels have wooden spokes, the men sit in the open, the cargo is uncovered. The Stroh's driver must climb up to his seat by a step hanging from the support beam, while the National Tea Company drivers swung up to their seats over the wheels and the shafts.*

## Detroit-Windsor Tunnel

*This is a good illustration of the difficulties of pinpointing the contents of a single photograph. The Michigan Central Railroad Company built a tunnel beneath the Detroit River in 1909–10. The city of Detroit built a tunnel in the late 1920s for automobiles. This photograph was placed in a file titled "Detroit-Windsor Tunnel." In which tunnel is this worker eating lunch?*

*The railroad tunnel was built because ferries could only transport a few freight cars across the river at a time, which created huge bottlenecks on either side of the river. In winter, with ice forming in the river, traffic jams were even worse. The tunnel, planners hoped, would smooth out these problems. The second tunnel was built for automobiles and to expand trade with Canada and the eastern coast of the United States.*

*In both cases, huge sections of the tunnel were made of reinforced concrete above ground, floated out to their positions and then sunk. Here, a tunnel worker opens a connection between one section and another. The doorway is in a half-finished state, with wood beams surrounding it and unconnected pipes nearby.*

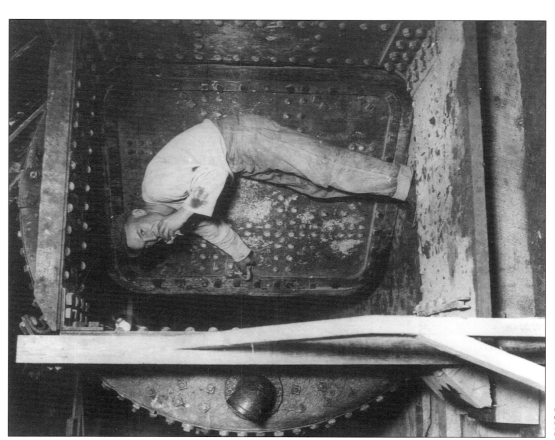

W26

## "Going up" on steelworkers' elevator

Industrialization had a different effect on the construction industry from the effect it had on automobile manufacturing. While Henry Ford and his contemporaries were devising the assembly line and eliminating most skilled jobs from the process of auto manufacturing, construction saw changes in its workforce, but not all construction work was deskilled. Engine-driven hoists, for instance, eliminated the need for unskilled carriers of bricks and mortar; the use of steel and reinforced concrete, on the other hand, reduced the demand for stonemasons but created a demand for skilled iron and cement workers.

Construction boomed in Detroit in the 1910s and 1920s. Downtown and the New Center area were the sites of most skyscraper building, including the Statler, the Tuller, the G.M. Building, the Penobscot Building, Cadillac Tower, the Fisher Building, and the Bell Telephone Building. At the same time, auto manufacturers built enormous complexes, like the Ford River Rouge plant and the Dodge Main factory. While the auto trades remained generally unorganized up until the mid-1930s, construction workers became the backbone of the American Federation of Labor's skilled trades unions. Even so, accident rates were hardly better in one industry than another: one historian estimates that construction workers on Detroit skyscrapers suffered one death per floor.

W27

# Community

By the 1920s, the city of Detroit sprawled miles from the city center. European immigrants lived in enclaves to the north, west, and south, while African-American migrants to the city were segregated into a section on the east side of downtown. Some felt the urban mélange was alienating, foreign, and dangerous. Others wrested from it a sense of community centered around neighborhood businesses, schools, churches, and movie theaters.

Above all, Detroit was a young town, teeming with children and young men and women. Industrial accidents, disease, impure food, and inadequately purified water reduced the chances of a Detroiter growing very old. Elementary school taught children basic reading, writing, and arithmetic skills. It also accustomed immigrant children to American life by teaching English, American history, and the national anthem. Some immigrants—Germans, especially—objected to the emphasis on English and American culture and erected private schools for their children instead. Public schools were imbued with Protestant teachings—teachers led classes in prayer and Bible readings. This also alienated some immigrants, especially the Catholic Irish and Poles. They turned to the Catholic Archdiocese for their children, and parish schools sprang up all over the city. The Tolkacz family, for example, sent their five children to Immaculate Conception's elementary school.

Yet children of varying backgrounds were not completely separate. Parks and playgrounds, organized and unorganized sports, movie theaters, and the streets themselves drew people from different ethnicities. Detroit Tigers fans, for instance, spanned age, gender, ethnicity, and social class. In this way, urban residents built a larger community as well as smaller, more local, communities.

While the Ford Sociological Department photographers sought to record the homes of company employees, and manufacturers used pictures to document the work in their factories, few city residents set out to chronicle the life of Detroit communities from 1900 to 1930. As many photographers have discovered, however, sometimes the most telling picture occurs by happenstance. Some of the photographs that best capture the community come from collections intended for other purposes. The twin brothers William H. and John J. Manning opened Manning Brothers Commercial Photographers in 1906. Hired by insurance companies to document the state of buildings and structures around Detroit, they also inadvertently documented the city and its people. Another photographer, Harvey C. Jackson, had a studio on Beaubien between Division and Adelaide, in Paradise Valley. He advertised his services as a portrait photographer, but also roamed the streets of the ghetto, taking pictures of children, school classes, and passersby. In addition, the Catholic Archdiocese of Detroit had photographs made to document new churches and parish halls; their photographers also captured settlement houses, tenements, and public celebrations. Once again, most of these photographs have never been published before.

This section starts with images of children and adolescents, then depicts the recreation and entertainment the city provided adults. We also see manifestations of religious impulses, from the hastily organized churches to the formal religious structures that attracted working-class Detroiters. Turning then to images of the city and its businesses, we explore both prosperity and poverty. The final images represent Detroit in the throes of the Great Depression, a turning point that marked the end of Detroit's first burst of phenomenal growth.

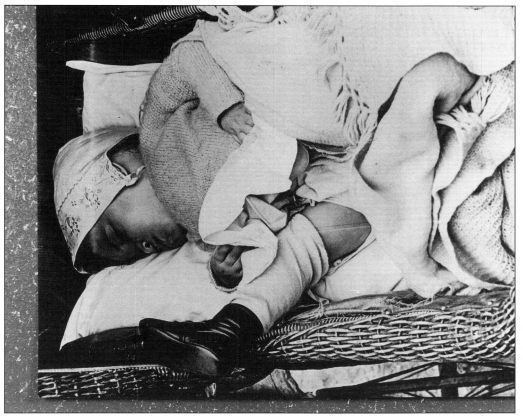

*C1   Child asleep, Detroit, 1920s.*

## Children playing on tenement roof, 1935

Spaces to play in the city were few and far between. City planners did not allot many areas for parks or playgrounds. Children had to make do with what was at hand. These children play on a tenement rooftop. With no play equipment in sight, the children must have played games like tag and hopscotch or imagined themselves defenders of a castle's ramparts or lookouts in the crow's nest of a ship. The photographer may have doled out the lollipops the young ones are enjoying as a reward for cooperating in his effort to capture one aspect of life in the city.

C2

## Children playing in a playground, c. 1935

*When playgrounds were available for local children, play equipment was often makeshift. Two girls make mud pies with old tin cans while the swingset, empty of swings, stands forlornly behind them. The children on the sawhorse seesaw have trouble balancing, even though a mother helps to steady the board. One-and two-family homes front onto this play area—the fence indicates that it is probably a schoolyard.*

## Two children outside their home
in Detroit, c. 1935

*It is symbolic, perhaps, that these children were found playing on old tires, a commodity the Motor City produced in abundance. Most Detroit children of the late 1920s played in streets and alley ways, and in the few playgrounds scattered through residential neighborhoods. Children might use the stoops for stoopball or the streets for skating or stickball (with telephone poles and manhole covers marking the bases). Sidewalks were the venue of games of marbles, jacks, or jumping rope. The temptations of the streets— the fruit stacked in front of the market, the opportunity to tease the junkmen and ragpickers, the footprints to be made in newly laid concrete—often brought children to the attention of the policeman patrolling on foot. More often than not, he would warn the child or inform the parents and do no more than keep a close eye on the miscreant in the future. Many upper-class Detroiters maintained that city streets were not a fit environment for young children, but most children made do with what they found.*

C4

## Two boys on a fence, c. 1935

*Playing hooky or hanging out on the corner after school? To a youth, the growing city of Detroit could be an exciting place, what with new models of cars to identify and marvel over, streetcars to ride (with or without paying), new construction to inspect, and so on. Since many boys left school when it was first legally permissible, at age fourteen, the years of freedom to roam the city must have seemed few indeed. When children left school at this age, they generally joined the factory workforce, thereby decreasing their leisure time but also increasing their wages and ability to enjoy what free time they did have.*

## Bishop School

Schooling in the early part of the century prepared children for their roles in later life. Boys, parents and teachers assumed, would work in the city's manufacturing industries. They needed practical training and mechanical abilities. Girls, on the other hand, would work in the home, either as housewives or as domestic servants. Schools accepted the sex-segregated world of industrial work and helped to reinforce sex-role socialization.

The young girls of Bishop School pictured here are learning about domestic work. Bishop School stood on Rivard, between Adelaide and Winder streets, on the edge of the area known as Black Bottom. A high proportion of African-American girls left school at a young age to become domestic servants. Wearing caps, aprons, and high button shoes, the girls stand in the front of a classroom. Each holds a doll and puts a finger to her lips to tell the viewer to be quiet for her sleeping charge. The dolls, of course, are all Caucasian.

## Weinman Settlement House, Larned and Orleans, founded 1908

Social settlements sprang up in most major American cities in the late nineteenth and early twentieth centuries. Pioneered in the United States by Jane Addams, settlements were intended as neighborhood centers, where local residents could socialize, take classes in home economics, and join discussion groups on politics, literature, or art. The middle-class women and men who lived in settlements reached out to the immigrants around them by offering aid in negotiating the ins and outs of local bureaucracies, serving as liaisons between immigrants and urban political structures, and as links between the poor and the rich.

In 1908, the League of Catholic Women of Detroit established the Weinman Settlement House at the corner of Larned and Orleans streets. Here, they pose with the sons and daughters of Italian and Middle Eastern immigrants who lived in the area, which is also depicted in several photographs taken by the Ford Sociological Department (see photos H8 and H21). These children may have been part of a kindergarten class offered at the settlement—kindergartens were not incorporated into public schools in Detroit in 1908—or they may have been members of a boys and girls club run by settlement residents. The settlement residents saw such endeavors as multipurpose. They kept children off the streets and out of trouble; they offered parents a form of child care; they offered children an introduction to American ways; they offered middle- and upper-class Detroiters assurances that an effort was being made to help the poor; and they demonstrated to city officials the importance of planned and supervised recreation for the young.

## Williams School

Two dolls enjoy their milk, just as these Williams School students enjoy their milk and crackers at snack time. Kindergarten teachers Louise Crockett and Margaret Robb emphasize nutrition instruction in their classes: "A Bottle a Day" and "We Need Milk" read the posters on the doors. The proportion of working-class children under five who died from diseases such as diphtheria, scarlet fever, pneumonia, and measles, and from diarrheal disorders brought on by improper nutrition was startlingly high in the first two decades of the century. In part, dietary problems were economic: in hard times, working-class families could not afford to feed all family members a balanced diet. In addition, inadequate knowledge of children's nutritional needs meant that children were fed starches and some meat, but few fruits and vegetables.

Middle-class public health reformers launched a two-pronged attempt to bring down the high rate of infant mortality. First, they attacked the problem of food purity. In the case of milk, they passed legislation to ensure that all milk was pasteurized and transported in refrigerated railroad cars. Second, they attempted to convey to the working class up-to-date nutritional information. This was best effected, reformers reasoned, by reaching them through their children. Hence the snacks and posters at Williams School.

Milk Distribution, Williams School, April 1921

## YMCA Boys Club Building, c. 1910

It seems that these boys were caught in the midst of showering. The photographer, however, may have staged this shot to show the spacious new facilities of the Metropolitan Detroit YMCA, built in 1909. The YMCA began its work in Detroit in 1864. By 1909, it had already outgrown three previous buildings in downtown Detroit. From its new quarters on Grand Circus Park, YMCA activities expanded and the organization opened new branches all over the city.

The YMCA in Detroit, like YMCAs in most large cities, had a number of interrelated goals. First, founders hoped to provide organized recreation for local boys. Recreational opportunities, they thought, would keep boys off the streets and off the path that would lead to jail. In addition, the YMCA carried out a program of Americanization efforts, reaching out to recent immigrants and their children. These boys might have attended a class or used the gymnasium during hours when it was open for local children.

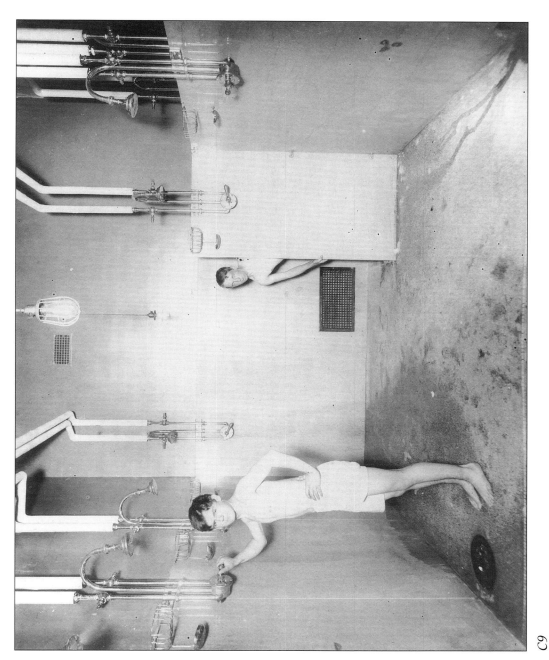

## YMCA

This group of boys used the downtown YMCA gymnasium three times a week. They were transported there from the Wayne County Detention Home, where children were housed prior to a hearing before the juvenile court. Children detained by police officers for committing crimes—girls were usually brought to court for being "incorrigible" (disobeying their parents) or for "committing sex crimes" (being sexually active), while boys usually were caught in some sort of petty thievery or burglary—were separated in the detention home by age and gender. "Dependent" children (those whose parents could not support them or who sent them out to beg) also were brought to the detention home.

This group was probably made up of delinquents and depen-dents; the older boys were almost certainly delinquents. Children detained by the police enjoyed the use of the YMCA gym for a few weeks until their cases were heard in court. At that point, the judge could send delinquent boys home on probation, or to any of a number of manual training schools. The judge usually placed dependent boys in various institutions or awarded state funds to the boys' mothers and sent the boys home.

## Purple Gang lineup, May 17, 1929

*Sometimes neighborhood gangs petered out as the boys grew older, and sometimes they grew into much more. Prohibition created the opportunity for a great deal of illegal liquor trafficking across the Detroit River and two "roughhouse" Jewish gangs dominated that trade in the mid-1920s. The Oakland Sugar House Gang and the Purple Gang members grew up together on the city's east side. They joined forces to manage the import of Canadian whiskey, which they repackaged under false labels and shipped to New York, St. Louis, Toledo, and to Al Capone's organization in Chicago. Legend has it that they dug a tunnel under the Detroit River to transport the whiskey and deployed speedboats on the river itself to act as decoys.*

*The Purple Gang had smaller operations, too—extortion of protection money, kidnapping, contract murders, and so on. The group's leaders were flamboyant, dressing fashionably and frequenting Detroit nightclubs (note the suits, shined shoes, and stylish fedoras). In 1929, however, when this photo was taken, the Purple Gang was sliding into oblivion: four members were sentenced to twenty-one months in prison; another member was sentenced to twelve years for manslaughter; and another was shot and killed by a rival gang.*

C11

## Hamtramck High football team, 1918

When the photographer took this portrait of the 1918 Hamtramck High football team, he arranged the players in the traditional pose of American sports teams. But the Hamtramck High team undoubtedly was not composed of traditional Americans. It is highly likely that most of the players were foreign-born or the sons of immigrants. Some of their parents may have wondered why their sons were devoting so much time and energy to a game when they could be earning valuable wages in the factories. First-generation American boys like these, however, did not see sports simply as a diversion. Football and baseball served as a bridge from their parents' world to mainstream American society.

Immigrant Poles—the majority of Hamtramck's residents—generally tried to build homogeneous ethnic enclaves. On the football team, their sons learned to work and play alongside a variety of people. Note the African-American player in the second row. As they traveled to games in other sections of the city, the players' world widened even more. Participating in sports could not completely separate these teenagers from their parents, however. Although they struck the poses of American sports heroes, their portrait was framed by slag heaps and factories, a physical reminder of the world their parents have built.

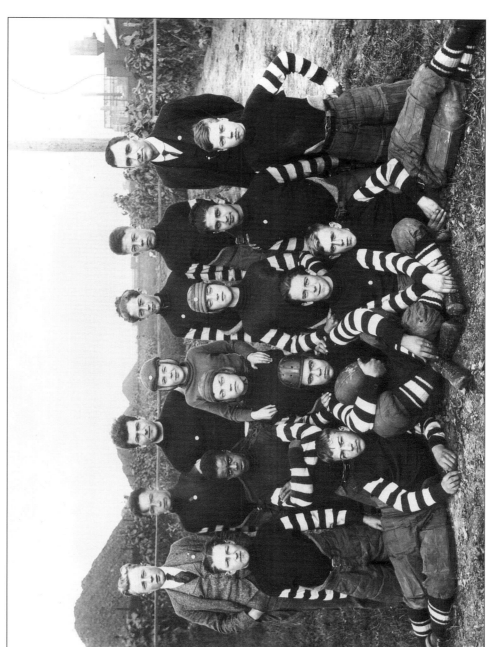

C12

## St. Rose of Lima graduating class, c. 1920s

*This high school graduating class is a study in the youth culture of the 1920s. The girls, by their dress, demonstrate their awareness of the fashions of the times. All but one of the girls has bobbed hair, some even have a permanent wave (it was called marcelled hair). Their skirts and dresses have hemlines just above the knee; their belts emphasize their waistlines, while the dress length emphasizes their legs and ankles. Although some of the girls wear a single strand of pearls, others wear a piece of male costume adapted for females, the tie. Some even wear both. The photo can't show us the details of the girls' faces—it looks like they are wearing lipstick, but are they also wearing rouge and powder? The practicality of the "new woman's" clothing, in addition to its provoking aspects, symbolized women's revolt against traditional constraints.*

*The boys at first glance seem less fashion-conscious. There they stand, in their suits and ties, foursquare and ready to face the world. Stacomb, a brand of hair cream, keeps even the curliest hair in place, while a pomade gives it luster. We can't smell the aftershaves or colognes they wore, so we will have to imagine them, instead. Catholic high schools of the 1920s were far from insulated against the shifting winds of fashion.*

C13

## Hastings Street

On a Sunday morning in the 1910s, a young woman walks down Hastings Street with her two young children. Returning from church, this woman reflects some of the more secular values of the age. She and her children are dressed in their best clothes; her ornate hat is testimony to her taste. Compare these children to those in photos C2 and C7. Clothes symbolize many things: taste, of course, and economic and social standing. For women earning their own wages, clothes symbolized freedom from paternal constraints. Clothes took on such an importance in the early part of the century, in fact, that young women often made sacrifices in other areas in order to dress well: they skipped meals, walked instead of using the streetcar, or stopped paying their rent. Similar sacrifices were made for all sorts of entertainment; to go to the dance, or the club, or the amusement park merited daily inconveniences.

In an area of the city characterized by extremely cramped apartments, the street took on a new importance. It became the venue for socializing, meeting members of the opposite sex, and dating. Both men and women promenaded on the street, displaying their taste in clothes and companions. To many young urban dwellers, walking on the street meant that they were under scrutiny. Two impoverished sisters in New York considered "their clothing [to be] so poor that they were ashamed to go out on Sunday—when everybody else put on 'best dresses'—and would sit in their room all day" (Peiss, p. 63).

## Parade, downtown Detroit, 1901

A moment of civic pride and display, this parade marked the two-hundredth anniversary of the founding of Detroit. An event of this sort gave residents a chance to display themselves in their finest, several hours of free entertainment, and a sense of community often hard to find in growing cities like Detroit. The men are wearing suits and straw boaters, the women are wearing shirt-waists and summer hats, and umbrellas shade the watchers from the sun or perhaps a light drizzle. Delivery boys from the grocery watch only a few paces from the dignitaries on the reviewing stand, across the street is the Detroit Opera House next to Wonderland, which boasts "continuous vaudeville theater."

The Common Council of the City of Detroit planned three days of events to commemorate the founding of the city by the French in 1701. On July 24, the mayor dedicated the new statue commissioned for the occasion, the Cadillac Chair or Chair of Justice, in Cadillac Square. On the second day, the women of the city—including women's sodalities from the Catholic churches—organized a floral parade. Friday, July 26, saw the allegorical display march through the city. Here, men dressed as French soldiers symbolize Cadillac's retinue as they pass through the Campus Martius.

In 1901, Detroit was still in the early stages of its phenomenal growth. In this photo, the skyline is low, but a tall building is going up beyond the Wonderland theater. Were the workers on those steel beams using their vantage point to watch the parade?

C15

## Tiger Stadium and crowds

When Frank Navin opened Navin field for the 1912 baseball season, the Detroit Tigers fielded an excellent team. Fans could watch Ty Cobb as he rapped out 227 hits and achieved a .410 batting average. In addition, there were powerful hitters like Davy Jones and Sam Crawford (Wahoo Sam); pitcher Wild Bill Donovan, shortstop Little Donie Bush, and catcher Oscar Stanage. During World War I, when this photo was taken, the team included Bernie Boland, Bobby Veach, Harry Heilman, and Oscar Vitt. Although the team went to the World Series in 1907, 1908, and 1909, it was never really in contention during the war years.

On this cold spring or late fall day, slush forms puddles on the walkway and fans have lit a fire to keep warm. These men and boys are willing to brave the cold to see their heroes play. They are also willing to pay, as the least expensive seat in the ballpark cost fifty cents, one-tenth of Ford's fabled five dollar day. Like all baseball fans, these people showed up out of a mixture of team loyalty, the opportunity for an afternoon's entertainment, and the fascination of the game itself. The team attracted interest from all the ethnic groups in the city: in 1908, for example, the immigrant Polish newspaper Dziennik Polski covered the Tigers' games in detail.

## Wildcat stands

By 1900, professional baseball was a big business. Star players received extraordinary salaries for their services: the Tigers' Ty Cobb, the greatest hitter of the day, reportedly earned $50,000 for the 1926 season, thirty times a typical autoworker's annual wage. Team owners like Detroit's Frank Navin traded on intense fan interest and generous government support to turn substantial profits. The billboards pictured here, positioned along the outfield wall so as to face the most expensive seats, provided just a small part of the Tigers' revenues.

Professional baseball was also a workingman's sport. Workers identified with players like Cobb, whose rough edges reflected their working-class backgrounds. Workers were less likely to identify with owner Navin, however. Rather than pay fifty cents for a stadium seat, Corktown residents built their own "wildcat" stands just beyond the outfield fence, where they could watch the games for free. Local politicians also took advantage of the view for some free advertising. The wildcat stands were not open to all, however. The crowd is exclusively male—imagine climbing that ladder in a skirt!

C17b

C17a

## Dreamland Cafe, High and Hastings streets, March 15, 1923

Beyond the bandstand and partially obscured by it sit a half dozen Caucasian men and women. Visiting the nightclubs in the black ghetto—or "slumming," as it was known—was a popular pastime among some middle- and upper-class whites in the 1920s. The Dreamland Cafe catered to well-to-do blacks: the women are in furs, the men's hair is marcelled, all the patrons are drinking whiskey or mixed drinks, even though Prohibition is in effect. The evening seems to be a slow night, however, as a number of tables are empty.

Segregated into the city's worst housing and barred from all but the lowest paying industrial jobs, African-American Detroiters found few avenues for upward mobility. Entertainment offered one path. Jazz and blues musicians who were trained in the brothels and honky-tonks of the South could find regular work, and regular paychecks, at the many clubs and cafes of Detroit's Paradise Valley—including, most famously, the Royal Garden and the

Graystone. Perhaps, with luck and hard work, a band might find backing to take their act to the centers of black music, the blues bars of Chicago's south side, for instance, or the theaters and ballrooms of Renaissance Harlem. Did the club's dancer also dream of success, or did she see a night of titillating the crowd simply as a way to pay her bills?

The Graystone, on Canfield and Woodward, catered to both blacks and whites. Blacks were allowed to dance starting at midnight, when the whites left. "We would crowd in there starting at midnight and dance till morning," one black Detroiter, M. Kelly Fritz, reminisced. St. Antoine Street drew the young revelers like a magnet. "There were all sorts of cafes and what-not there. If it were a weekend, we'd go on to a morning dance," he went on. "It was called a breakfast dance. After having danced the night before you'd think we would have had enough, but it was quite the contrary" (quoted in Moon, p. 81).

THE DREAMLAND CAFE
ENTERTAINMENT AND DANCING
COR. HIGH AND HASTINGS ST.

C18

## 2840 Hastings Street, interior of a bar, 1938

*A shot and a beer was the standard fare in this Hastings Street bar. Men who stopped by after work might also make the lunch counter their regular haunt at midday. What appears, at first, to be a homogeneous group of men reveals itself, upon a second examination, as an extremely stratified and differentiated collection. The men at the bar are drinking and generally seated alone (note the man with crutches); the men at the tables eat as well as drink and sit in groups. The white male contingent is clustered in the center of the room; two black men sit near the door, clearly separate from the whites. The only women in the establishment are employees. The white women serve at the bar, while the black woman works in the tiny kitchen selling chili. Black-owned chili parlors dotted Detroit in the 1920s; in this case, one business had found a niche inside another.*

## Interior of the Cozy Theater, 1922

In the early years of the twentieth century, a new form of entertainment burst into the lives of working-class Detroiters. Silent movies attracted middle- and working-class people alike, including the multitude of immigrants and their children, who could understand the pictures (although not, perhaps, the captions) even if they understood little else of American life. Families often attended together; children, according to several studies, made up between a quarter and a half of movie audiences. At a nickel a show, movies were affordable and popular, contributing to the growth of the leisure industry.

The aptly named Cozy Theater was typical of the hundreds of small storefront theaters that dotted the streets of working-class neighborhoods. Its cramped, unpretentious quarters boasted egalitarian seating and offered its neighbors a place for informal socializing, eating, and drinking. It also offered teenagers a cover of darkness for their "socializing." The silent movies also offered audiences an interactive entertainment, as children read the movie captions aloud and translated for their parents, adults commented on the action, babies cried, and the piano player entertained during and after movie showings.

C20

## WWI soldiers marching to train station in Detroit, 1917

As Walter I. McKenzie marched off to World War I, were his thoughts on the familiar Detroit streets or on the family he left behind? The latter, apparently. He had this photo made into a postcard which he sent to his parents, indicating the captain of his company so that they could see the man who would lead their son into battle.

The soldiers, with the recruits behind them, passed through the streets on their way to the Detroit train station. From there they travelled to a training camp and thence to Europe. Although the year is 1917, early in American involvement in the war, reaction to the soldiers is mixed. Spectators on the right side of the street seem focused on the column of men, while the men on the left side of the street seem to be passing the time of day. Some young workers in the Jemson Building watch from the second-floor windows, perhaps wondering whether they should enlist.

C21

## Bus on Eleven Mile/Woodward (Royal Oak)

This photo captures the transition between different worlds: between the horse-drawn age and the horseless; between the urban and suburban; between the era of servants and the home of modern conveniences. The bus on Eleven Mile Road and Woodward Avenue traversed the streets of Royal Oak, a rural area slowly becoming suburbanized. The passengers (all male) wear boaters and long dusters, just as they would if they occupied a horse-drawn carriage. Note the black servant who watches the bus.

Royal Oak would not long remain the placid rural community it appears to be in this photo. By the early 1920s, industrial workers—many of them of immigrant stock—began to move into the area. The influx of newcomers horrified many native-born residents, who feared the immigrants would destroy the town's rural character. The tension exploded in 1926. The Detroit Catholic Archdiocese had recently opened a parish at Woodward and Twelve Mile Road. Many residents saw the presence of a new Catholic church as an indicator of the invasion of the foreign-born. Two weeks after the completion of the church, on a hot night in July, the Knights of the Ku Klux Klan burned a cross on the parish lawn, terrorizing the pastor, the young Father Charles Coughlin, and his staff. The peace of the countryside, it is clear, had been lost forever.

C 22

## Altar set up in movie theater, n.d. (pre-1920)

The massive influx of working people into Detroit between 1910 and 1920 strained many of the city's institutions. Detroiters adapted as best they could, turning poolrooms into boarding-houses, schools into social centers. No transformation was more profound, though, than the one pictured here. On Saturday night, workers young and old crowded into the theater to laugh at, cheer, and jeer the latest movie. The next morning, many of the same workers, dressed now in the formal clothes of the devout, returned for Sunday mass.

Detroit had always had a large Catholic population, and the diocese maintained an extensive complex of churches, schools, and convents. Even that complex of institutions could not meet the spiritual needs of the thousands of Poles, Italians, and Croats who poured into the city in search of work after the turn of the century. The diocese tried to keep up: between 1910 and 1930, it founded 107 parishes in the metropolitan area. But church leaders simply couldn't build churches fast enough to meet the demand. Parishes thus improvised, temporarily transforming neighborhood stores, homes, and even theaters into sacred spaces.

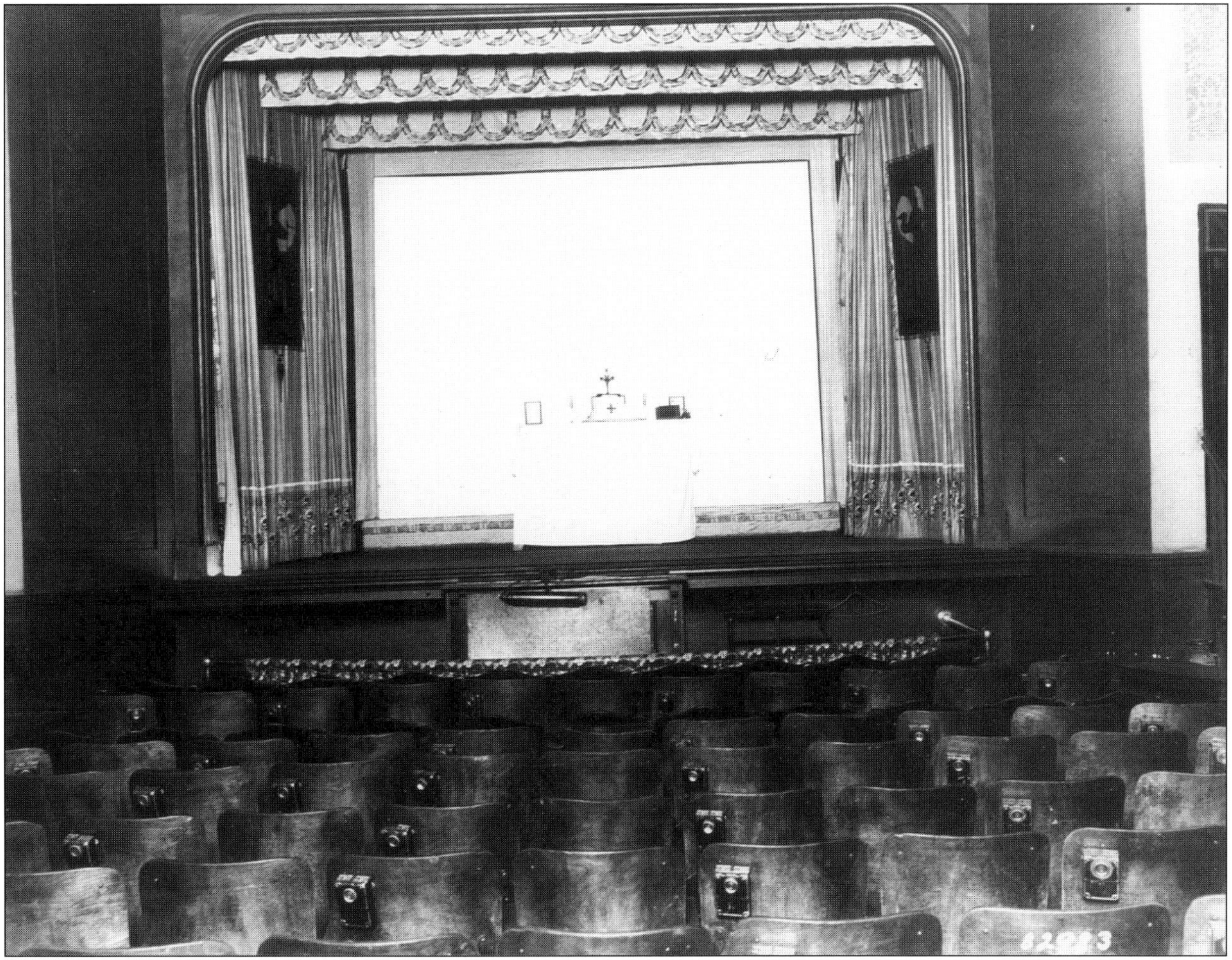

*C23*

## May Procession, Detroit

The two young girls who watched this procession probably would not participate in the same rituals when they grew up. This May procession of a Catholic women's sodality reinforced the Old World traditions with which these women had been raised. Marching under a banner depicting the Pietà, this group was probably a sodality honoring the Virgin Mary. Most of the activities of the sodalities—prayer and socializing—took place in the church, but at regular intervals they took the church to the streets.

Such processions died out as the twentieth century progressed. The confraternities (men's groups) and sodalities no longer play a central role in most Catholic churches. For the moment, however, the activities of the parish dominate the eastern and southern European immigrant neighborhoods in the city.

## Dedication of St. Rose of Lima church, September 26, 1920

*The schoolboys perched on the ledge of the partially constructed building watch as Bishop Michael J. Gallagher dedicates the new church in 1920. Dressed in the uniform of the school behind them, they embody the priorities of the Catholic parishes in the booming metropolis: the school building was standing and in operation before the cornerstone of the church was laid. The two events were not long distant, however, as the parish itself had been established only the year before.*

*The crowd is intent on the church dignitaries. The policemen stationed in front of the platform gaze at the crowd impassively. Just as the women's sodalities took the church to the streets, here the congregation is in the street for the purpose of enclosing itself in a building that would symbolize the parish's strength.*

C25

## Funeral rites and ceremonies, n.d.

*Working-class Americans lived under the shadow of death. Industrial accidents claimed many working people in the prime of life; the rigors of childbirth killed many working-class women; and poor sanitation and inadequate diets pushed up the mortality rate for children and the aged. That certainly seems to be the case here. Though it is impossible to tell the age of the deceased, it may be that the young woman to the right of the casket is his widow, the child standing forlornly in front of her his son. Conversely, the deceased could be a child and the woman his or her mother.*

*Working-class Detroiters—like their compatriots across industrial America—dealt with their losses by ritualizing death, often at great expense. Eastern European immigrants, like those pictured here, typically hired an undertaker to prepare the deceased for burial. Bereaved family members made sure their loved ones were laid out in ornate caskets, while friends and neighbors sent elaborate and expensive floral displays to the family; to do anything less was to dishonor the dead. The body lay in state, usually at home, for three or four days. At least one member of the com-*

*munity, and often more than one, sat with the body the entire time. That responsibility normally fell to men, who often had to skip work, and thus forego their wages, to fulfill their obligations. Friends, neighbors, and coworkers were also expected to attend the funeral service and to accompany the family to the gravesite, which the family would have chosen with care, securing the best possible location in the cemetery. "Work, work," a Polish mother constantly told her daughter, "and earn for your grave" (Cohen, p. 65).*

*The very existence of this photo attests to the importance of these rituals. Family members went to the expense of hiring a photographer and endured the trouble and pain of standing for the photo in order to document the impressive number of people who attended the interment. It is easy to imagine the photo occupying a place of honor in the bereaved's home on Franklin Street and to imagine her sending a copy to her family in Europe as proof that even in a strange land her she was a member of a community that mourned with her.*

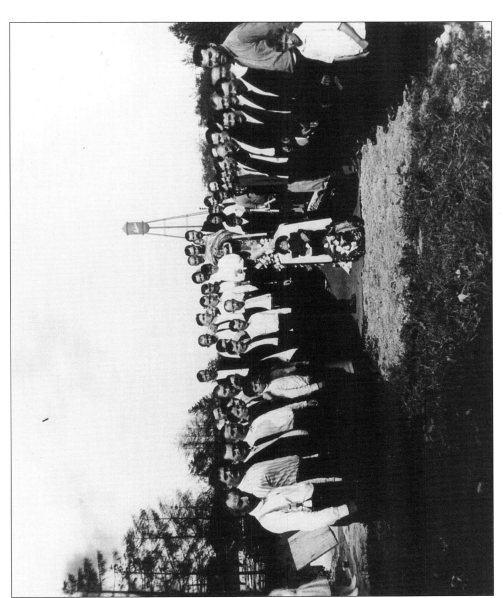

C26

## Bethel A.M.E.

"Bethel Social Service" reads the sign over the doorway, welcoming migrants from the South. Realizing that the huge numbers of African-American migrants coming from Georgia, Mississippi, Alabama, and other southern states would need aid adjusting to Detroit, Bethel A.M.E. members established a social service department in 1911 and a labor and housing bureau shortly thereafter. These bureaus helped those in need find jobs and housing; they also helped bring new members to the already thriving black church. In 1919, the church had 2,737 members. In 1926, it had 3,500.

Like most African Methodist Episcopal churches, Bethel's congregation was very involved in running the church. The biennial rotation of ministers reinforced the laymen's importance in the church. In this photo, taken in front of the building on the corner of Napoleon and Hastings, the minister is not clearly identified by dress or position—indeed, he may be absent from the picture entirely. Bethel served the middle class of the African-American community in Detroit, while St. Matthew's Episcopal church served the upper class (including many of the trustees of the Dunbar Memorial Hospital) and Second Baptist and any number of storefront fundamentalist churches served the lower classes.

Some 70 percent of Bethel A.M.E.'s membership was female. The majority of these women were housewives, and only a small proportion were working women. The black churches attracted women by serving as the venue for female benevolent society meetings. The church basements were used, at one point, as public schools for black children, while the chapels and church halls were the site of political meetings.

# Old bearded man on Hastings Street, February 13, 1927

Between 1900 and 1914, Detroit's Jewish population grew by twenty-four thousand. Mass immigration from Russia and Eastern Europe started in the 1880s and reached epic proportions by the turn of the century. Jews were escaping poverty, restrictions on their ability to choose a place to live, on movement within Europe, on their ability to own property and to send their children to school. Russian pogroms—state-sanctioned mob terrorism against Jews—spurred thoughts of di goldene medine, "the golden land": America.

Eastern European Jews generally came to Detroit after living some time in the United States. They were attracted by its plentiful jobs, parklike boulevards, and relatively clean and spacious—compared to New York City's tenements—housing. The influx of Jews sparked fears among Detroiters of disease, crime, and the destruc-

tion of America's "grand Christian civilization" (Rockaway, p. 52). Notwithstanding nativist attacks, the city's Jewish population continued to grow, settling into an area centered on Hastings Street on Detroit's east side.

This old man paces along Hastings in 1927. In his lifetime, he had immigrated to America and come to live in Detroit. He had also traversed some of the greatest gaps in the century: from horse-drawn carts to streetcars and automobiles, from candlelight to electric light, from local entertainment to the radio and the movie theater. But not everything in his life had changed. In Detroit, this man could still eat kosher food, speak Yiddish with his neighbors, go to the temple for services, read Hebrew newspapers. Residence in the United States also gave him the opportunity to own a business, to settle where he wished, and invest in his children's education.

C28

## Overhead view of Jefferson Avenue, February 28, 1919

*When this photograph was taken on February 28, 1919, the Jefferson Avenue–Connor Avenue neighborhood was a major manufacturing site. Several thousand men and women worked in the Chrysler Corporation, Hudson Motor Car Company, and Briggs Body plants in the area, and thousands of others worked in the small parts plants that dotted the streets leading down to the Detroit River.*

*Such activity leaves its mark on the landscape. A pall of smoke obscures the rows of tightly packed houses in the distance. Jefferson Avenue itself was dominated by businesses catering to factory hands. There are at least six restaurants, where workers could get a quick bite and perhaps a surreptitious beer; in the two blocks closest to the photographer. The Hotel Hudson appeals to the suitcase brigade by playing on the name of one of the neighborhood's largest employers.*

## Hastings Street by Kirby and Florence, 1922

In a typical example of neighborhood and ethnic succession, this area of Hastings Street became a center of Russian-Jewish settlement in Detroit in the 1880s. As the Jewish community moved north, the black community expanded in its wake, so that forty years later, Hastings Street formed the nucleus of Paradise Valley, the black ghetto. Even so, in 1922, when this photo was taken, evidence of Jewish settlement yet abounded. Not only are the people in the street white, but the two storefronts visible are Robinowitz's Poultry and Fish Market and Katovitsky's Meat Market, both undoubtedly kosher. In addition, tailoring was one of the most typical occupations of immigrant Jews. What are the indications that this is an African-American area as well? Perhaps the billboard, with its figure of a black girl, perhaps the barbershop, as barbering was a common occupation for black men in Northern cities.

Jews and African Americans in Detroit had generally cordial relations in the 1920s. Recently, a black migrant to Detroit from Georgia gave a mental tour of Hastings Street as he remembered it in the 1920s. On one corner, William Hines recalled, "was a baker's shop. At the end of evenings, if there were any bagels left over, we got them" (quoted in Moon, p. 77).

## Exterior of the Clairmont Theater, 12th Street and Clairmont, 1928

In 1928, the storefronts along Twelfth Street ranged from luncheon places to conservatories of music. They included a newsstand, above that Morris Schwartz's dental office, the 12th-Clairmont Market run by Peter Con, an empty storefront that had been a children's clothing shop, a lunch place advertising steak and chips, Velick Brothers' shoe store, Block and Pupko's clothing store, the Clairmont theater; A. Pupko's Dress Goods, a branch of the Bank of Detroit, Clark's laundry, the European Conservatory of Music, and across the street a store advertising sewing machines. These storefronts provide a number of clues to the character of the neighborhood and the street itself; Twelfth is one of the main business streets in the neighborhood, and the neighborhood has a mixture of middle- and working-class residents. The second floors of these buildings housed an occasional apartment and the offices of physicians, lawyers, and dentists.

The people who walked down Twelfth in the 1920s, who weighed themselves on the scale in front of the newsstand, whose children bought gumballs from the machines on the street, were primarily Anglo-Saxon. They were middle-level office white-collar workers and managers, and some skilled and semiskilled workers. By the late 1940s, the area was dominated by African-American residents. In fact, it was here, on the corner of Twelfth and Clairmont, that the 1967 riot began.

## Street scene: Erskine and Rivard, April 12, 1929

During the 1950s, the center of the black ghetto in Detroit was paved over to become an interstate freeway. In 1929, the corner of Erskine and Rivard was only a block from the main thoroughfare of the ghetto, Hastings Street. As they flooded into the city from the South, African Americans settled in transitional neighborhoods, neighborhoods that were not very cohesive and, in general, had a high proportion of Russian Jews. By 1920, the ghetto, nicknamed Black Bottom or Paradise Valley, covered an area bounded by the river on the south, Farnsworth on the north, Hale Street and Elmwood Cemetery on the east, and St. Antoine Street on the west. Jews lived in the area surrounding Hastings Street to the north and an Italian neighborhood bordered the ghetto on the east.

Paradise Valley earned a reputation as a center of vice and prostitution, but on this day the photographer found a very ordinary scene. In the afternoon of April 12, 1929, the street is already beginning to take on the aspects of a hot summer's day. The women are wearing short sleeved dresses, the windows of the buildings are open, the man on the corner has loosened his tie. The boy in the street is barefoot, although poverty may be more involved in this case than the heat.

C32

## Communist (union) rally in downtown, March 5, 1930

Fifty thousand demonstrators gathered in downtown Detroit on March 5, 1930, in response to a Communist Party call for world-wide protests against unemployment. The U.S. Communist Party was one of the forces behind protests against bad working conditions and no working conditions in the 1920s and 1930s. In 1930, the United States was sinking ever deeper into the Great Depression: the economy slowed to a halt, men and women were out of work, charities were overwhelmed with requests for aid, and the government did nothing, confident that the situation would right itself.

Unemployment in Detroit was terrifyingly high as automobile manufacturers cut production in response to declining demand for new cars. Between 1929 and 1931, for example, the Ford Motor Company slashed its workforce by ninety-one thousand people— about 71 percent of its payroll. In addition, auto companies reduced the wages of those who retained their jobs by about 50 percent, while prices in the city dropped by only 20 percent.

The city reacted harshly to the protest. Three thousand police-men ringed the demonstrators around City Hall and Woodward Avenue. Mounted police rode into the crowd and attacked with clubs, sending twenty-two men and women to the hospital. The men and women in this picture listen to speakers in the calm before the storm. Note that the crowd includes both workingmen and white-collar workers; there are several men (organizers, perhaps) wearing suits and ties.

C33

## Voting booth, 1932

When these voters lined up to cast their ballot this grim November day in 1932, national concerns had overwhelmed local issues. Detroit's economy had been in a desperate spiral for more than three years. More than a quarter of the city's workers were unemployed, thousands were evicted from their homes each week, and one hospital reported treating four cases of starvation every day. The very future of the nation seemed to hinge on the outcome of the presidential election.

Detroit's white workers had typically supported the Democratic party in the early twentieth century. They did so largely because local Democrats seemed more sensitive than the Republicans to their immediate needs. A Democratic alderman might be able to find an unemployed workingman a city job, a practice Republicans often frowned upon; a local saloon keeper knew the Democratic councilman would approve his liquor license,

whereas the Republican was likely to support Prohibition. Black Detroiters, on the other hand, had overwhelmingly supported the Republican party, seeing in the Democrats the party of white supremacy.

The Depression changed the rules of working-class politics. Local Democrats simply did not have the resources to meet the needs of the city's unemployed, while the national Republican party, led by Herbert Hoover, refused to commit the federal government's resources to the crisis. In desperation, white and black workers both threw their support to the national Democratic party and its candidate, Franklin Delano Roosevelt. It was a risk. FDR had offered voters nothing more than the vague promise of a "new deal." But at least that promise gave workers some hope for better days ahead. And on a grim November day in 1932, hope was all that many workers had.

C34

## Homeless men eating at Fisher Lodge, November 12, 1931

When the Great Depression started, unemployed men and women turned first to their families for assistance. When whole families became impoverished and homeless, they looked to churches and local charities for food and shelter. Families split apart, as each member was forced to fend for him or herself. Men "rode the rails" by the hundreds, hoping to find a meal or day labor in the next town, or at least a place where they could sleep for a few pennies a night. The men pictured here found standard depression fare—soup and coffee, and maybe some bread—served at the city-run Fisher Lodge for the unemployed.

"I have never confronted such misery as on the zero day of my arrival in Detroit," social worker Helen Hall wrote in 1930. At the Department of Public Welfare, she stated, she came upon crowds thronging the hallways: each man and woman was there to find help for their families. "I wanted to look at them and see what type of men and women they really were, but I was ashamed to look" (quoted in Holli, p. 170).

The story of the Great Depression and its impact on Detroit is another story altogether from the one explored here. It is fitting, then, to end with this image.

# Bibliography

Abraham, Sameer Y., and Nabeel Abraham, eds. *Arabs in the New World: Studies on Arab-American Communities*. Detroit: Wayne State University Press, 1983.

Adams, Myron. "The Housing Awakening: A City Awake—Detroit." *Survey* (August 5, 1911): 666–71.

Anderson, William N. *The Detroit Tigers: A Pictorial Celebration of the Greatest Players and Moments in Tigers' History*. South Bend, Ind.: Diamond Communications, 1991.

Babson, Steve. *Building the Union: Skilled Workers and Anglo-Gaelic Immigrants in the Rise of the UAW*. New Brunswick, N.J.: Rutgers University Press, 1991.

Babson, Steve, with Ron Alpern, Dave Elsila, and John Revitte. *Working Detroit: The Making of a Union Town*. New York: Adama, 1984.

Bailer, Lloyd. "Negro Labor in the Automobile Industry." Ph.D. diss., University of Michigan, 1943.

Barnes, James. *Wealth of the American People: A History of Their Economic Life*. New York: Prentice-Hall, 1949.

Bodnar, John. *The Transplanted: A History of Immigrants in Urban America*. Bloomington: Indiana University Press, 1985.

Bolkosky, Sidney. *Harmony and Dissonance: Voices of Jewish Identity in Detroit, 1914–1967*. Detroit: Wayne State University Press, 1991.

Brinkley, Alan. *Voices of Protest: Huey Long, Father Coughlin and the Great Depression*. New York: Vintage, 1983.

Cohen, Lizabeth. *Making a New Deal: Industrial Workers in Chicago, 1919–1939*. Cambridge: Cambridge University Press, 1990.

Common Council of the City of Detroit. *The Bi-centenary of the Founding of the City of Detroit 1701–1901*. Detroit: n.p., 1902.

Denby, Charles. *Indignant Heart: A Black Worker's Journal*. Boston: South End Press, 1978.

*Detroit City Directory*. Detroit: R. L. Polk, 1900–1929.

Dunbar Memorial Hospital. *Biennial Report, 1930–31*. Detroit: n.p., n.d.

Elkholy, Abdo A. *The Arab Moslems in the United States*. New Haven, Conn.: College and University Press, 1966.

Engelmann, Larry. *Intemperance: The Lost War against Liquor*. New York: Free Press, 1979.

Ewen, Stuart. *Captains of Consciousness: Advertising and the Social Roots of the Consumer Culture*. New York: McGraw-Hill, 1976.

Fass, Paula S. *The Damned and the Beautiful: American Youth in the 1920's.*

New York: Oxford University Press, 1977.

Ferry, W. Hawkins. *The Buildings of Detroit: A History*. Detroit: Wayne State University Press, 1980.

Fine, Sidney. *The Automobile under the Blue Eagle: Labor, Management, and the Automobile Manufacturing Code*. Ann Arbor: University of Michigan Press, 1963.

Finkel, Kenneth. *Nineteenth Century Photography in Philadelphia*. New York: Dover, 1980.

Fox, Richard Wightman, and T. J. Jackson Lears, eds. *The Culture of Consumption*. New York: Pantheon, 1983.

Gabin, Nancy F. *Feminism in the Labor Movement: Women and the United Automobile Workers, 1935–1975*. Ithaca, N.Y.: Cornell University Press, 1990.

Gamble, Vanessa N. *The Black Community Hospital: Contemporary Dilemmas in Historical Perspective*. New York: Garland Publishers, 1989.

Hales, Peter B. *Silver Cities: The Photography of American Urbanization, 1839–1915*. Philadelphia: Temple University Press, 1984.

Hall, Helen. "When Detroit's Out of Gear." *Survey* 64 (April 1, 1930): 9–14, 54. Reprinted in *Detroit*, ed. Melvin G. Holli. New York: New Viewpoints, 1976.

*Helpful Hints and Advice to Employes: To Help Them Grasp the Opportunities Which Are Presented to Them by the Ford Profit-Sharing Plan*. Detroit: Ford Motor Company, 1915.

Higham, John. *Strangers in the Land: Patterns of American Nativism*. New Brunswick, N.J.: Rutgers University Press, 1955.

Hudson, James J. *Hostile Skies: A Combat History of the American Air Service in World War I*. Syracuse, N.Y.: Syracuse University Press, 1968.

Ihlder, John. "Booming Detroit." *Survey* (July 29, 1916): 449–50.

Katzman, David M. *Before the Ghetto: Black Detroit in the Nineteenth Century*. Urbana: University of Illinois Press, 1973.

Kirkland, Edward. *Industry Comes of Age: Business, Labor, and Public Policy, 1860–1897*. New York: Holt, Rinehart, and Winston, 1961.

Kleinberg, S. J. "Death and the Working Class." *Journal of Popular Culture* 11:1 (1977): 193–209.

———. *The Shadow of the Mills: Working-Class Families in Pittsburgh, 1870–1907*. Pittsburgh: University of Pittsburgh Press, 1989.

Klinkenborg, Verlyn. *The Last Fine Time*. New York: Vintage, 1990.

LaGumina, Salvatore J., and Frank J. Cavaioli. *The Ethnic Dimension in American Society*. Boston: Holbrook Press, 1974.

Leake, Paul. *History of Detroit: A Chronicle of Its Progress, Its Institutions, and the People of the Fair City of the Straits*, vol. 1. Chicago: Lewis Publishing, 1912.

Lesy, Michael. *Bearing Witness: A Photographic Chronicle of American Life, 1860–1945*. New York: Pantheon, 1982.

Levine, Robert M. "Semiotics for the Historian: Photographers as Cultural Messengers." *Reviews in American History* 13 (1985): 380–85.

Lewis, David L. *The Public Image of Henry Ford: An American Folk Hero and His Company*. Detroit: Wayne State University Press, 1976.

Lichtenstein, Nelson. "Life at the Rouge: A Cycle of Workers' Control." In *Life and Labor: Dimensions of American Working Class History*, Charles Stephenson and Robert Asher, eds. Albany: State University of New York Press, 1986.

Lichtenstein, Nelson, and Stephen Meyer, eds. *On the Line: Essays in the History of Auto Work*. Urbana: University of Illinois Press, 1989.

Marquardt, Frank. *An Auto Worker's Journal: The UAW from Crusade to One-Party Union*. University Park: Pennsylvania State University Press, 1975.

Mason, Gregory. "Americans First: How the People of Detroit Are Making Americans of Foreigners." *New Outlook* (September 27, 1916): 193–96, 200–201. Reprinted in *Detroit*, Melvin G. Holli, ed. New York: New Viewpoints, 1976.

Mason, Philip P. *The Ambassador Bridge: A Monument to Progress*. Detroit: Wayne State University Press, 1989.

Meier, August, and Elliot Rudwick. *Black Detroit and the Rise of the UAW*. New York: Oxford University Press, 1979.

Meyer, Stephen III. *The Five Dollar Day: Labor Management and Social Control in the Ford Motor Company, 1908–1921.* Albany: State University of New York Press, 1981.

Milkman, Ruth. *Gender at Work: The Dynamics of Job Segregation by Sex during World War II.* Urbana: University of Illinois Press, 1987.

Montgomery, David. *The Fall of the House of Labor: The Workplace, the State, and American Labor Activism, 1865–1925.* New York: Cambridge University Press, 1987.

Moon, Elaine Latzman. *Untold Tales, Unsung Heroes: An Oral History of Detroit's African American Community, 1918–1967.* Detroit: Wayne State University Press, 1994.

Nelson, Daniel. *Managers and Workers: Origins of the New Factory System in the United States, 1880–1920.* Madison: University of Wisconsin Press, 1975.

Nevins, Allan, and Frank Ernest Hill. *Ford: Expansion and Challenge, 1915–1933.* New York: Charles Scribner's Sons, 1957.

Norman, Hans, and Harold Runblom. *Transatlantic Connections: Nordic Migration to the New World after 1800.* Oslo: Norwegian University Press, 1988.

North, Douglass. *Growth and Welfare in the American Past: A New Economic History.* 2nd ed. Englewood Cliffs, N.J.: Prentice-Hall, 1974.

Norton, Mary Beth, et al. *A People and a Nation: A History of the United States.* 1st ed. Boston: Houghton Mifflin, 1982.

Nowak, Margaret Collingwood. *Two Who Were There: A Biography of Stanley Nowak.* Detroit: Wayne State University Press, 1989.

Oestreicher, Richard. *Solidarity and Fragmentation: Working People and Class Consciousness in Detroit, 1875–1900.* Urbana: University of Illinois Press, 1986.

Orton, Lawrence. *Polish Detroit and the Kolasinski Affair.* Detroit: Wayne State University Press, 1981.

Peiss, Kathy. *Cheap Amusements: Working Women and Leisure in Turn-of-the-Century New York.* Philadelphia: Temple University Press, 1986.

Peterson, Joyce Shaw. *American Automobile Workers, 1900–1933.* Albany: State University of New York Press, 1987.

Petruck, Peninah R. *The Camera Viewed: Writings on Twentieth-Century Photography.* New York: Dutton, 1979.

*Photography Rediscovered: American Photographs, 1900–1930.* Essay by David Travis. New York: Whitney Museum of Modern Art, 1979.

Riess, Steven. *City Games: The Evolution of American Urban Society and the Rise of Sports.* Urbana: University of Illinois Press, 1989.

Riis, Jacob. *How the Other Half Lives: Studies among the Tenements of New York.* 1890; rpt. New York: Sagamore Press, 1957.

Rockaway, Robert A. *The Jews of Detroit: From the Beginning, 1762–1914.* Detroit: Wayne State University Press, 1986.

Rosenzweig, Roy. *Eight Hours for What We Will: Workers and Leisure in an Industrial City, 1870–1920.* New York: Cambridge University Press, 1983.

Schneider, John C. *Detroit and the Problem of Order, 1830–1880: A Geography of Crime, Riot, and Policing.* Lincoln: University of Nebraska Press, 1980.

Stark, George. *City of Destiny: The Story of Detroit.* Detroit: Arnold Powers, 1943.

Stricker, Frank. "Affluence for Whom? Another Look at Prosperity and the Working Classes in the 1920s." In *The Labor History Reader,* Daniel J. Leab, ed. Urbana: University of Illinois Press, 1985.

Sward, Keith. *The Legend of Henry Ford.* New York: Rinehart, 1948.

Tentler, Leslie Woodcock. *Seasons of Grace: A History of the Catholic Archdiocese of Detroit.* Detroit: Wayne State University Press, 1990.

———. "Who Is the Church? Conflict in a Polish Immigrant Parish in Late Nineteenth Century Detroit." *Comparative Studies in Society and History* 25 (1983): 241–76.

Thomas, Richard W. *Life for Us Is What We Make It: Building Black Community in Detroit, 1915–1945.* Bloomington: Indiana University Press, 1992.

# Bibliography

Trachtenberg, Alan. *Reading American Photographs: Images as History, Mathew Brady to Walker Evans.* New York: Hill and Wang, 1989.

Turner, Peter, ed. *American Images: Photography 1945–1980.* London: Viking, 1985.

Tyack, David. *The One Best System: A History of American Urban Education.* Cambridge: Harvard University Press, 1974.

U.S. Bureau of the Census. *Fifteenth Census of the United States, 1930.* Washington, D.C.: Government Printing Office, 1937.

U.S. Census Bureau. *Twelfth Census of the United States, 1900* vol. 1. Washington, D.C.: U.S. Bureau of the Census Office, 1901.

U.S. Department of Commerce. *Statistical Abstract of the United States, 1933.* Washington, D.C.: Government Printing Office, 1933.

Welling, William. *Collectors' Guide to Nineteenth-Century Photographs.* New York: Macmillan, 1976.

Zunz, Olivier. *The Changing Face of Inequality: Urbanization, Industrial Development, and Immigrants in Detroit, 1880–1920.* Chicago: University of Chicago Press, 1982.

# Photo Credits

H1: Ford Motor Company Industrial Archives, acc. AR–84-57033, photo 308.

H2: Burton Historical Collection of the Detroit Public Library, Harvey C. Jackson Collection.

H3: Ford Motor Company Industrial Archives, acc. AR–84-57033, photo 347.

H4: Ford Motor Company Industrial Archives, acc. AR–84-57033.

H5: Ford Motor Company Industrial Archives, acc. AR–84-57033.

H6: Ford Motor Company Industrial Archives, acc. AR–84-57033, photo 343.

H7: Ford Motor Company Industrial Archives, acc. AR–84-57033, photo 294.

H8: Ford Motor Company Industrial Archives, acc. AR–84-57033, photo 421.

H9: Ford Motor Company Industrial Archives, acc. AR–84-57033, photo 583.

H10: Ford Motor Company Industrial Archives, acc. AR–84-57033, photo 417.

H11: Ford Motor Company Industrial Archives, acc. AR–84-57033, photo 418.

H12: Ford Motor Company Industrial Archives, acc. AR–84-57033, photo 416.

H13: Ford Motor Company Industrial Archives, acc. AR–84-57033, photo 341.

H14: Ford Motor Company Industrial Archives, acc. AR–84-57033, photo 339.

H15: *Detroit News*, Catlin Photo Album, Historical Album of Detroit, vol. 3.

H16: *Detroit News*.

H17: Ford Motor Company Industrial Archives, acc. AR–84-57033, photo 358.

H18: Ford Motor Company Industrial Archives, acc. AR–84-57033.

H19: Ford Motor Company Industrial Archives, acc. AR–84-57033, photo 423.

H20: Ford Motor Company Industrial Archives, acc. AR–84-57033, photo 344.

H21: Ford Motor Company Industrial Archives, acc. AR–84-57033, photo 425.

H22: Ford Motor Company Industrial Archives, acc. AR–84-57033, photo 423.

H23: Ford Motor Company Industrial Archives, acc. AR–84-57033, photo 299.

W1: Henry Ford Museum and Greenfield Village.

W2: The Archives of Labor and Urban Affairs, Wayne State University.

W3: Ford Motor Company Industrial Archives, acc. AR–79-31632:2.

W4: The Archives of Labor and Urban Affairs, Wayne State University.

W5: Ford Motor Company Industrial Archives, acc. AR–79-31632:2.

W6: Henry Ford Museum and Greenfield Village.

W7: The Archives of Labor and Urban Affairs, Wayne State University.

W8: The Archives of Labor and Urban Affairs, Wayne State University.

W9: Ford Motor Company Industrial Archives, acc. AR–79-31632:2, photo 7 (#40) 82204 in corner.

W10: The Archives of Labor and Urban Affairs, Wayne State University.

W11: The Archives of Labor and Urban Affairs, Wayne State University.

W12: Michigan Historical Collections, Bentley Library, University of Michigan, Carey Pratt McCord Collection.

W13: Manning Brothers Historical Collection, grocery stores file, photo 16684.

W14: Michigan Historical Collections, Bentley Library, University of Michigan,

YMCA of Metropolitan Detroit.

W15: Michigan Historical Collections, Bentley Library, University of Michigan, YMCA.

W16: Michigan Historical Collections, Bentley Library, University of Michigan.

W17: Michigan Historical Collections, Bentley Library, University of Michigan, Charles William Ungermann Collection.

W18: Burton Historical Collection of the Detroit Public Library.

W19: Tom Featherstone, private collection.

W20: Henry Ford Museum and Greenfield Village.

W21: Manning Brothers Historical Collection, Streetcar #1 file, photo 30091.

W22: Manning Brothers Historical Collection, Jefferson Ave. file, photo 33828.

W23: Michigan Historical Collections, Bentley Library, University of Michigan, William Christian Weber Collection, Box 26, Ambassador Bridge file.

W24: Michigan Historical Collections, Bentley Library, University of Michigan, Christian T. Fedderson Collection, National Tea Co. file, 1950.

W25: Michigan Historical Collections, Bentley Library, University of Michigan, Stroh Brewery Company.

W26: Michigan Historical Collections, Bentley Library, University of Michigan, William Christian Weber Collection, Box 26, Detroit-Windsor Tunnel file.

W27: *Detroit News.*

C1: Burton Historical Collection of the Detroit Public Library, Harvey C. Jackson Collection.

C2: Archdiocese of Detroit Archives, League of Catholic Women Collection, Box 51.

C3: The Archives of Labor and Urban Affairs, Wayne State University.

C4: The Archives of Labor and Urban Affairs, Wayne State University.

C5: The Archives of Labor and Urban Affairs, Wayne State University.

C6: Burton Historical Collection of the Detroit Public Library, Harvey C. Jackson Collection.

C7: Archdiocese of Detroit Archives, League of Catholic Women Collection, Box 51.

C8: Burton Historical Collection of the Detroit Public Library, Harvey C. Jackson Collection.

C9: Michigan Historical Collections, Bentley Library, University of Michigan, YMCA of Metropolitan Detroit, Box 3, Boys Club Building 1900–1910s file.

C10: Michigan Historical Collections, Bentley Library, University of Michigan, YMCA of Metropolitan Detroit, Box 3, Boys Club Activities file.

C11: *Detroit News,* Gangs—Purple—Detroit file.

C12: Manning Brothers Historical Collection, Sports file, photo 26854.

C13: Archdiocese of Detroit Archives, St. Rose of Lima Collection, Box 11.

C14: Burton Historical Collection of the Detroit Public Library, Harvey C. Jackson Collection, Bands file.

C15: Henry Ford Museum and Greenfield Village.

C16: Ernie Harwell Sports Collection of the Burton Historical Collection.

C17: Ernie Harwell Sports Collection of the Burton Historical Collection.

C18: Manning Brothers Historical Collection, Black History file, photo 2429.

C19: Manning Brothers Historical Collection, Bars file, photo 130553.

C20: Manning Brothers Historical Collection, Theaters C file, photo 45550.

C21: Michigan Historical Collections, Bentley Library, University of Michigan, Walter I. McKenzie Collection, Military Service file.

C22: Michigan Historical Collections, Bentley Library, University of Michigan, George Thorne Collection, Automobiles and Motoring file.

C23: Archdiocese of Detroit Archives, pre-church worship sites.

C24: Michigan Historical Collections, Bentley Library, University of Michigan, Topical Photo Collection, Box 1, Ethnicity file.

C25: Archdiocese of Detroit Archives, St. Rose of Lima Collection, Box 11.

C26: Burton Historical Collection of the Detroit Public Library.

C27: Burton Historical Collection of the Detroit Public Library, Harvey C. Jackson Collection.

C28: *Detroit News,* Jews—Detroit file.

C29: Manning Brothers Historical Collection, Jefferson Ave. file, photo 96907.

C30: Manning Brothers Historical Collection, Black History file, photo 47314.

C31: Manning Brothers Historical Collection, Theaters C file, photo 89078.

C32: Manning Brothers Historical Collection, Black History file, photo 99606.

C33: *Detroit News,* Communists—Detroit—Prior to 1932 file.

C34: *Detroit News,* Detroit Elections—Voting Booth file.

C35: *Detroit News,* Unemployment—Detroit 1930–39 file.